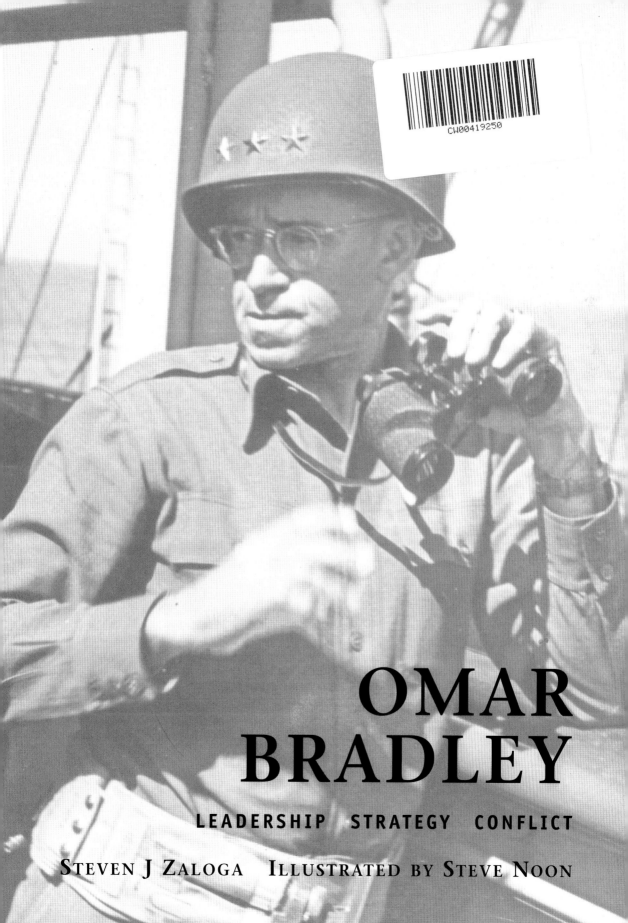

OMAR BRADLEY

LEADERSHIP   STRATEGY   CONFLICT

STEVEN J ZALOGA   ILLUSTRATED BY STEVE NOON

First published in 2012 by Osprey Publishing
Midland House, West Way, Botley, Oxford OX2 0PH, UK
44-02 23rd St, Suite 219, Long Island City, NY 11101, USA

E-mail: info@ospreypublishing.com

Print ISBN: 978 1 84908 660 8
PDF e-book ISBN: 978 1 84908 661 5
EPUB e-book ISBN: 978 1 78096 418 8

Editorial by Ilios Publishing Ltd, Oxford, UK (www.iliospublishing.com)
Cartography: Mapping Specialists Ltd.
Page layout by Myriam Bell Design, UK
Index by Sandra Shotter
Originated by PDQ Digital Media Solutions Ltd, Suffolk, UK
Printed in China through Worldprint Ltd.

12 13 14 15 16 10 9 8 7 6 5 4 3 2 1

A CIP catalog record for this book is available from the British Library.

Artist's note

Readers may care to note that the original paintings from which the
color plates in this book were prepared are available for private sale.
All reproduction copyright whatsoever is retained by the Publishers.
All Inquiries should be addressed to:

Steve Noon, 50 Colchester Avenue, Penylan, Cardiff, CF23 9BP, UK

The Publishers regret that they can enter into no correspondence upon
this matter.

Front-cover image

NARA

The Woodland Trust

Osprey Publishing are supporting the Woodland Trust, the UK's leading
woodland conservation charity, by funding the dedication of trees.

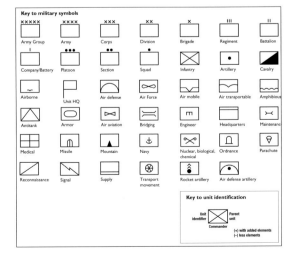

CONTENTS

INTRODUCTION

An official portrait of Lt. Gen. Omar N. Bradley taken in the winter of 1945 following the Ardennes campaign. (NARA)

Omar Bradley commanded the largest US Army formation to see combat in World War II. Although Bradley was the most significant American tactical commander in the European Theater of Operations (ETO), George S. Patton has overshadowed him in the public mind. Bradley started the war in Patton's shadow, serving as his deputy in North Africa and commanding a corps during the campaign on Sicily. The controversies surrounding Patton on Sicily derailed his chances for further advancement, and Bradley's calm professionalism led to his selection to head the main US Army force in Normandy, the First US Army. Following Bradley's well-executed breakout from Normandy, he was elevated to command the enlarged 12th Army Group which included Patton's Third US Army. Bradley's greatest challenge came in December 1944 when the Germans launched an unexpected counteroffensive in the Ardennes. Although Bradley's reputation suffered from his failure to anticipate the German attack, his prudent planning and foresight helped to exploit the tactical windfall provided by the unexpected capture of the Rhine bridge at Remagen in March 1945. This shifted the focus of Allied operations in the final month of the war, with Bradley's 12th Army Group playing the central role in the final campaign into Germany. Bradley executed the greatest encirclement operation of the war, the envelopment of Heeresgruppe B in the Ruhr pocket. Bradley served as the chairman of the US Joint Chiefs of Staff in the early years of the Cold War, including the tumultuous years of the Korean conflict.

THE EARLY YEARS

Omar Nelson Bradley was born on February 12, 1893 to John and Sarah (Hubbard) Bradley in Randolph County, Missouri. He was named after the local newspaper editor,

Omar D. Gray, a family friend. The Bradley family traced their roots back to Britain in the mid-1700s, first emigrating to Madison County, Kentucky. His paternal grandfather, Thomas Bradley, was a private in the Confederate States Army during the Civil War, though his maternal grandfather had served in the Union Army. The family moved to the Missouri territory early in the 19th century, settling in the farm country near Clark and Higbee. Bradley's ancestors for the most part were sodbusters – poor farmers and sharecroppers working the land on the Great Plains. Bradley's father had greater ambitions and after a great deal of self-education, he qualified as a rural schoolteacher. Bradley later described him as "a curious blend of frontiersman, sportsman, farmer, and intellectual," an avid baseball player and enthusiastic hunter. Bradley picked up many of his own enthusiasms from his father, both his intellectual curiosity and his skill with a baseball bat and a .22-cal. rifle. His upbringing was fairly typical of poor farm kids on the Great Plains. He accompanied his dad to school, and being too poor to own a horse, they walked several miles every day back and forth to the rural classroom. Whatever meat was on the family table came from hunting, and the young Bradley contributed by plinking frogs with his BB gun, and later squirrels with his prized .22-cal. rifle. Bradley was an intelligent and self-motivated student and he was usually at the top of his class. His father died prematurely in January 1908 from pneumonia, placing even greater strains on the family's meager resources. In the winter of 1909 at the age of 17, Bradley collided with another ice skater on a Moberly park, smashing his front teeth and gums. His family was too poor to permit any dental work, and the damage from this accident helps account for Bradley's glum visage, as he avoided smiling due to the "jumbled mess" of his front teeth. The situation deteriorated over the years and while stationed at Ft. Leavenworth in 1928, he had to have all his front teeth removed.

Bradley graduated from Moberly High School in 1910 at the top of his

A family portrait of Omar Bradley at age seven with his mother Sarah and father John Bradley. (MHI)

Bradley was an enthusiastic sportsman when young and captain of the Moberly High School baseball team of 1908. (MHI)

class and captain of the school's baseball and football teams. He hoped to pursue further education with the aim of becoming a lawyer. The family lacked the money for such an education, and so he decided to work in the boiler shop of the Wabash Railroad until he could save sufficient funds. A family friend casually mentioned that he might pursue a free government education by attending the US Military Academy at West Point.

THE MILITARY LIFE

Bradley had never seriously imagined a military career, and was motivated more by the prospect of a free education, much the same as another West Point classmate, Dwight Eisenhower. He applied for a nomination from his local congressman, but was informed that another student, Dempsey Anderson, had already been nominated. He was offered a slot as an alternate candidate and in the event Anderson failed while Bradley passed the grueling exams. He was ordered to report to West Point in August 1911. West Point at the time was quite small with only 265 freshmen and a Corps of Cadets of only 600 young men. Bradley's Class of 1915 proved to be "the Class the Stars fell on." Of the 265 plebes who arrived in the summer of 1911, 59 eventually became generals and two, Bradley and Eisenhower, won five stars. Bradley proved to be an able though unexceptional student though his skills at baseball earned him a spot on the varsity baseball team in 1912. The military academy stressed the role of sports in fostering group cooperation and, curiously enough, all the members of the 1914 baseball team went on to become generals. Bradley graduated from West Point as the 44th out of a class of 164; he later admitted that he might have displayed a better academic record with more study and less sports. When submitting his choices for service branches, he selected engineers, field artillery, and infantry in that order, as the two first branches had the reputation for prompter career advancement. In the event, he was offered an infantry slot and reported to the 14th Infantry in September 1915 at Ft. George Wright near Spokane, Washington. He was taken under the wing of Lieutenant Edwin Harding, a graduate of the West Point Class of 1909, who sponsored an informal gathering of unit officers to further their education in tactics and military history.

The Great War, which was taking place in Europe at the time, had little influence at the remote posts in the American Northwest, but the border troubles with Mexico soon attracted the Army's attention. In May 1915, the 14th Infantry was ordered to the Mexican frontier as part of General "Black Jack" Pershing's "Punitive Expedition."

Cadet Omar N. Bradley in front of his locker at the US Military Academy, West Point. (MHI)

The transfer temporarily delayed Bradley's marriage to his high-school sweetheart, Mary Quayle, which was postponed until January 1917. After the hostilities with Mexico cooled and the United States became involved in the European conflict, Bradley hoped to transfer to a unit more likely to be dispatched to France. Instead, in January 1918 Bradley's battalion was deployed to the copper-mining region near Butte, Montana, where the "Wobblies" (International Workers of the World) threatened to shut down the Anaconda mines which the federal government had deemed vital to the war effort. Bradley was appointed commander of Company F and his unit was assigned to maintain the peace in this violent frontier town. By August 1918, Bradley had been given a temporary rank of major. In September 1918, the 14th Infantry was consolidated at Camp Dodge in Iowa as part of the effort to mobilize the 19th Division for deployment to France. In the event, the unit was so hobbled by the Spanish influenza that it remained in camp until after the war's end.

Bradley's portrait in the West Point yearbook on his graduation. The accompanying text was written by classmate Dwight Eisenhower, the beginning of a long professional friendship. (MHI)

In July 1919 Bradley was ordered to report to San Francisco to lead a battalion destined for duty with the US Army in Vladivostok, part of the Allied effort to tip the balance in the Russian Civil War against the Communists. Bradley again missed combat when he was held back from deployment to serve on a court-martial. Bradley realized that the peacetime army would likely suffer from calamitous cutbacks, and sought a posting as a Reserve Officer Training Corps (ROTC) instructor. He served in this position in the summer of 1920 before being ordered to return to West Point as a mathematics instructor. Another prominent World War II commander, Matthew Ridgway, was transferred at the same time and their paths would cross often in the ensuing years. Such a posting was a considerable honor in the greatly diminished army of 1921, and Bradley served at a time when the academy was undergoing considerable turmoil because the new superintendent, Douglas MacArthur, had instituted a reform program at the famed institution. Omar and Mary Bradley abstained from much of the social life at the post; both were from strict Midwest Christian backgrounds and did not drink or smoke. This did not stop Bradley from becoming involved in the local poker games, regarding his skill at cards as a useful way to supplement his meager captain's income. Their first child, Elizabeth Bradley, was born while they were stationed at West Point.

Following the usual army career template, Bradley was expecting an overseas posting after finishing his four-year tour at West Point, most likely to Puerto Rico. However, his fellow instructor Matthew Ridgway broke the mold and received an assignment for the senior officers' advanced course at the Army's new Infantry School program at Ft. Benning. Major Bradley followed suit and attended in 1924. He graduated second in the class behind

Bradley on a picnic in 1915 with his sweetheart and future wife Mary Quayle. (MHI)

Bradley's tour as an instructor in the Weapons Course at the Infantry School at Ft. Benning in 1930–31 was a critical step in his career due to his contact with George Marshall. The instructors are pictured here: (back row, left to right) Howard Liston, Omar Bradley, Emil Leard, and Freemont Hodson; (front row) M. C. Stayer, Joseph Stilwell, George C. Marshall, W. F. Freehoff, and E. F. Harding.

Leonard "Gee" Gerow, who would lead V Corps under Bradley's command two decades later at Omaha Beach. Following his successful academic pursuits, Bradley returned to a more usual Army career track and in 1926 he was pleased to be assigned to Hawaii rather than Puerto Rico. Placed in command of the 1st Battalion, 27th Infantry, he found the post to be a congenial environment to put his Infantry School training into practice. Both the brigade and regimental commanders in Hawaii were veterans of the American Expeditionary Force in France in 1918, but neither was wedded to static trench warfare doctrine. They were impressed that Bradley had graduated with distinction from the recent Ft. Benning course, and they were also convinced that these Pacific duty posts were in the front line of any future conflict with Japan. Hawaii allowed Bradley to practice the type of fire-and-movement tactics taught at Ft. Benning in a real three-dimensional world and not simply as an academic exercise. Hawaii also served as the first contact between Bradley and Major George S. Patton, then the Hawaii Division's G-2 (intelligence officer). Patton and his wife were wealthy patrons of the social life on post, but the Bradleys with their quiet Midwestern upbringing and lowly social roots were uncomfortable with Patton's circle. By this stage Bradley had become an avid golfer, but Patton favored the expensive luxury of horses and disdained golf. Patton recruited Bradley for a trap-shooting team, and found him to be a crack shot. A bit prudish,

Bradley was upset by Patton's fluorescent profanity when speaking to the troops. Hawaii was the beginning of an important but troubled relationship between the two future commanders.

Bradley might have remained in Hawaii for another year or more but he feared that his proposed appointment as a liaison officer between the Regular Army and the local National Guard would be a drag on his future career prospects. He pressed for an appointment to the Command and General Staff School at Ft. Leavenworth, an inevitable stepping-stone for higher command positions. Bradley viewed the Ft. Leavenworth interlude as perfunctory ticket-punching to advance his career, and found the courses to be dull and unimaginative. On completing his courses, he was offered the posts of treasurer at West Point or instructor at Ft. Benning. Although his wife preferred the comfort of the Military Academy, Bradley preferred the challenge of the Infantry School. It proved to be one of his most important and influential decisions.

Colonel George C. Marshall was in charge of the Infantry School's curriculum. Marshall had been the operations officer of the 1st Division in France in 1918, and then on the staff of "Black Jack" Pershing's American Expeditionary Force headquarters planning the St. Mihiel offensive. His impressive performance in this campaign prompted Pershing to appoint him as chief of operations of the First US Army in October 1918 and he ended the war as chief-of-staff of VIII Corps. Bradley later characterized Marshall as "one of the greatest military minds the world has produced."

Bradley as a young officer in the 14th Infantry in Arizona in 1916 as part of Black Jack Pershing's Mexican Punitive Expedition. (MHI)

Even though Marshall was well experienced in static trench warfare, he was a firm believer in the future of maneuver and firepower as the pillars of modern battle. Marshall adopted a more radical teaching approach at Ft. Benning, no longer issuing the officers a set of detailed instructions for them to carry out, but rather providing a tactical problem which they had to solve using their own initiative. Marshall was a ruthless task-master, and more conservative officers who could not adapt to his demanding new style of command were sacked. Bradley was highly impressed with this approach, and it would strongly affect his own command style in dealing with subordinate commanders in the ETO in 1944–45. Of the 80 officers attached to the school, Bradley's performance was so outstanding that he was selected by Marshall as one of the handful assigned to top slots, in his case the chief of the weapons section which dealt with heavy infantry weapons including the machine gun, mortar and antitank gun. Bradley's Ft. Benning years also saw other young officers fall into Marshall's orbit. Captain Walter Bedell "Beetle" Smith was so outstanding in one of Bradley's classes, that Bradley asked Marshall's permission to appoint him as an instructor. Marshall

Bradley was an instructor in the Tactical Department at West Point in 1934–38 and is seen here quizzing a cadet. (MHI)

was surprised by Bradley's request because "Beetle" had "all the charm of a rattlesnake." Marshall entered both Bradley and Smith's names in his "little black book" of promising young officers. In later years after he became Army chief-of-staff, Marshall would pick "Beetle" Smith when Eisenhower needed an executive officer for the supreme command headquarters; Bradley was also on an upward trajectory under Marshall's keen eye.

On completing his Ft. Benning assignment, Bradley considered another step forward in his military education at the Army War College at Ft. Humphrey outside Washington, DC. The Infantry School commandant, General Joseph "Vinegar Joe" Stilwell, recommended against it, arguing that the War College simply prepared staff officers who would never command tactical formations. But his old friend Forest Harding convinced him that the Army was changing its ways and that attendance at the Army War College was a critical stepping-stone to high command. After a short interlude directing Civilian Conservation Corps public works teams, Bradley reported to the War College in 1933. He was unimpressed with the curriculum, finding it stodgy and pedestrian compared to the more dynamic example of the Infantry School. Past contacts on Patton's skeet-shooting team helped direct him to his next assignment when Colonel Simon Bolivar Buckner, the new commandant of cadets at the Military Academy, invited Bradley back to West Point to teach in the Tactical Department. Bradley spent most of 1934–38 training future officers at West Point. He was especially keen on promoting more realistic training, shepherding his students on field trips to Forts Benning and Monroe in the summer months, and exposing them to the new combat arms including tanks, antiaircraft, and Army aviation units. Bradley's students included many officers who would be battalion and regimental commanders in World War II. Bradley hoped to be appointed commandant of cadets at the end of his four-year tour, but the new superintendent pushed for his own choice.

Instead, Bradley was ordered to Washington to serve in the War Department as the assistant G-1, the personnel division. While not as prestigious as either G-2 (intelligence) or G-3 (operations), the position was well suited to Bradley's personal history of tours at the Army's various training establishments and his extensive personal contact with much of the inter-war army officer corps. When George Marshall was appointed chief-of-staff in April 1939, he immediately plundered the G-1 office and assigned Bradley to a small, handpicked "secretariat" under Orlando Ward that served as his administrative brain trust. It was up to the secretariat to weed out the trivial from the steady flow of documents and directives, and to distill them into action directives for Marshall's approval. This placed

Bradley at the center of Army policy-making in the months before the start of World War II in Europe, Marshall was convinced that the United States would be dragged into the European war, and strove to prepare the US Army for this eventuality in the face of a severely restricted budget and an isolationist Congress.

When Bradley's tenure on the general staff neared its end, he was slotted to take over the commandant of cadets post at West Point he had sought a few years earlier. By this stage in his career it was a lateral move, not an advancement. Marshall was unenthusiastic about wasting his talents and instead steered him to command the Infantry School at Ft. Benning. In February 1941, Bradley was promoted to brigadier general, the first officer from the Class of 1915 to receive a general's star. When assigned to the school, Bradley faced some daunting problems. With war on the horizon, the US Army was undergoing a hasty expansion of its strength with plans to triple its size by the middle of 1941. Such an effort required at least 100,000 new officers. A provisional scheme for new Officer Candidates Schools was already in place but was insufficient to the task. Bradley devised an "assembly line" approach that was widely ridiculed in Washington as little more than a factory for "90-day wonders." Marshall understood the practical necessity for the scheme, and approved it in spite of objections from his own G-1 office. Besides this innovation, Bradley changed the core curriculum at the Infantry School to integrate tanks, airborne forces, and air power into the training regime. One of his most ardent supporters became George Patton, who had resurfaced as a vigorous advocate of tanks following his assignment to senior command in the new 2nd Armored Division. Bradley's tenure at the Infantry School was curtailed by Marshall, who continued to steer him to higher commands. In the autumn of 1941 during a visit to the Infantry School, Marshall suggested that Bradley start grooming a successor as he planned to shift him to a divisional command. Bradley was still commanding the Infantry School on December 7, 1941 when Japan attacked Pearl Harbor.

In late December, Bradley was given a temporary rank of major general and sent off to reactivate the 82nd Division. The division had had a distinguished record in World War I as part of the American Expeditionary Force and its most famous member had been the legendary Medal of Honor winner Alvin York. The division was rebuilt around a small core of peacetime regular officers and enlisted men, but the majority of its troops were new draftees. Bradley created an effective training regime aimed at converting the raw recruits into effective soldiers in the minimum amount of time. He was with the 82nd Division for

Bradley's first division command in 1942 involved the formation of the new 82nd Division and he is seen here in 1942 during a tactical exercise. (MHI)

Bradley was an excellent marksman from his days hunting frogs and other small game with a BB gun, and he is seen here on the pistol range during the formation of the 82nd Division in 1942. (MHI)

only about four months when Washington shifted him to the 28th Division. This was a National Guard division, recruited in Pennsylvania. The National Guard divisions proved to have some inherent organizational and training issues that sharply degraded their performance, and there was a move by Washington in 1942 to clear up these problems before the divisions were committed to combat. Many of the senior officers were political appointees and were often overage and unfit for tactical command. Small units in the division were usually recruited from the same localities, led by officers who were prominent local citizens. While this "hometownism" was acceptable in peacetime it led to numerous problems in wartime, and Bradley immediately took steps to remedy the problem by reassigning troops throughout the division. Bradley's success in making both of these divisions battleworthy was noted by Marshall and the head of the Army Ground Forces (AGF), General Lesley McNair. In early 1943, Washington planned to elevate Bradley to command X Corps in Austin, Texas. This appointment lasted for hardly a day when Bradley received a phone call cancelling it. For security reasons, the AGF officer cryptically told Bradley: "Remember your classmate? You're going to join him." The classmate was Dwight Eisenhower, and Ike had asked for Bradley to help bolster his command staff after the disasters at Kasserine Pass.

THE HOUR OF DESTINY

Bradley immediately traveled to Washington to be personally briefed by George Marshall. The situation was grim: the US Army's II Corps had been subjected to a surprise attack near Sidi-bou-Zid in Tunisia on February 14 and sent reeling back towards the Kasserine Pass. While the lines had finally stabilized, the poor performance of II Corps demanded drastic action. Bradley arrived at the Allied Forces Headquarters (AFHQ) in Algiers on February 24, 1943 towards the culmination of the Kasserine Pass fighting. He was warmly greeted by Eisenhower, who viewed him as a dependable friend even though they had had only sporadic contact during the interwar years.

One of the first administrative requirements was to clear Bradley to read the Ultra decrypts of German radio traffic. Ultra was the most important Allied intelligence breakthrough of the war, but signals intelligence could be a double-edged sword. Eisenhower was very critical of its role in the Kasserine

Pass debacle. The AFHQ G-2, Brigadier E. E. Mockler-Ferryman, concluded that the main German intention was an attack by 5. Panzerarmee through the Fondouk Pass which would threaten the flank of British units in northern Tunisia. In spite of tactical intelligence pointing to intentions against the American II Corps, Mockler-Ferryman ignored this threat and as a result, II Corps was strung out in a series of weak outposts when the Germans struck. As effective as Ultra could be, it was by no means totally reliable. In the case of the German offensive, the Allied signals intelligence units had picked up only a small fraction of the German communications, and unfortunately only the

early discussions for Operation *Kuckucksei*, correctly assessed as a potential offensive against the British forces in northern Tunisia. This plan was quite controversial among the German commanders in the Mediterranean theater, and in the event, it was cancelled in favor of Operation *Frühlingswind*, the attack against II Corps at Sidi-bou-Zid. This later conversation between senior German commanders was invisible to Ultra as much of it was transmitted using secure codes or via transmissions other than radio. Although US II Corps intelligence picked up ample local evidence of German activity in its sector, this was largely ignored by AFHQ G-2 due to its faith in the early, though incomplete, Ultra decrypts. The Ultra controversy was an eye-opening experience for Bradley, who was completely unaware of Allied signals intelligence effort, and who was largely unprepared for the important role that Ultra would play in the forthcoming Allied campaigns in the Mediterranean Theater of Operations (MTO) and the subsequent European Theater of Operations (ETO). Intelligence controversies would continue to dog Bradley through his career.

Bradley began his tour in Tunisia in February 1943 as an aide to Eisenhower, but was soon attached to Patton's new II Corps Headquarters.

As Eisenhower's aide, Bradley had the usual ceremonial duties and is seen here reviewing French colonial troops with Gen. Henri Giraud, the head of the French Army in North Africa. (MHI)

Ike told Bradley that he wanted him to serve as his "eyes and ears" at the front. Bradley was uneasy with this mission, realizing that many would view him as the chief prosecutor in a witch-hunt to find scapegoats for the Kasserine debacle. This opinion was not dispelled after he met with Eisenhower's deputy theater commander, Gen. Harold Alexander, at his Constantine HQ. Alexander was the senior British land commander in the Mediterranean and he had already advised Ike to dump the American II Corps commander, Lt. Gen. Lloyd Fredendall, and his immediate

Bradley and his II Corps Headquarters staff in Tunisia in April 1943 with a sign reading "Situation Wanted: Rome–Berlin–Tokyo." (MHI)

superior, British Lt. Gen. Kenneth A. N. Anderson of First Army. Serious command changes were obviously underway, and Bradley had been thrown into the middle of the controversy without an adequate background of the issues. He traveled to II Corps' HQ with Ike's chief-of-staff, Gen. Walther Bedell "Beetle" Smith, a colleague from his Infantry School days. Both Bradley and Beetle were thoroughly unimpressed with Fredendall, even though he had the reputation of being one of Marshall's "Golden Boys." The II Corps HQ was located far behind the lines and Fredendall's staff was rabidly anti-British. Bradley fully agreed with Ike's policy that the forthcoming campaigns would be joint coalition efforts, and the vociferous attitudes of Fredendall and his staff against Anderson and senior British commanders were incompatible with this mission, no matter whether they were justified or not. Bradley and Beetle both agreed that Fredendall had to be relieved, and the matter was settled following a visit by another Eisenhower confidant, Maj. Gen. Ernie Harmon of the 2nd Armored Division, who categorized Fredendall as a "physical and moral coward."

Ike wanted to replace Fredendall with his old friend Mark Clark, but Clark had already been assigned to lead the Fifth US Army and saw the offer as a demotion. Ike instead turned to the other corps commander in theater, George Patton of I Armored Corps, who enthusiastically accepted the challenge. At first, Eisenhower planned to attach Bradley to Patton's II Corps HQ as an informal observer, but Patton correctly saw him as "Ike's spy" and suggested that he take on the more formal role of deputy corps commander. Ike agreed, and both men departed to lead II Corps in its further campaigns in Tunisia.

Bradley had never been particularly fond of Patton from their occasional personal contacts in the inter-war years. They were polar opposites in personality and had serious differences in their approach to command and leadership. Patton was egocentric, hyperactive, aggressive, and vulgar; Bradley was calm, quiet, self-effacing, and polite. Patton grew up in a family with considerable wealth and was an avid polo player and horseman; Bradley grew up in poverty and enjoyed the common man's sports of baseball and hunting. Patton had a romantic view of war, avidly sought situations to display his bravery, and craved glorious victories. Bradley saw himself as an honorable professional but lacked Patton's heroic obsessions. Patton wore a custom uniform and stood out in any group of officers; Bradley wore unadorned battledress and was indistinguishable from any other officer on his staff. When Patton took over II Corps, he instituted a set of draconian practices to instill martial spirit in the troops, including fines for not wearing helmets and ties even in the most incongruous circumstances. Bradley thought the same results could have been achieved by "more mature" measures.

II Corps in Tunisia, April 23–May 9, 1943

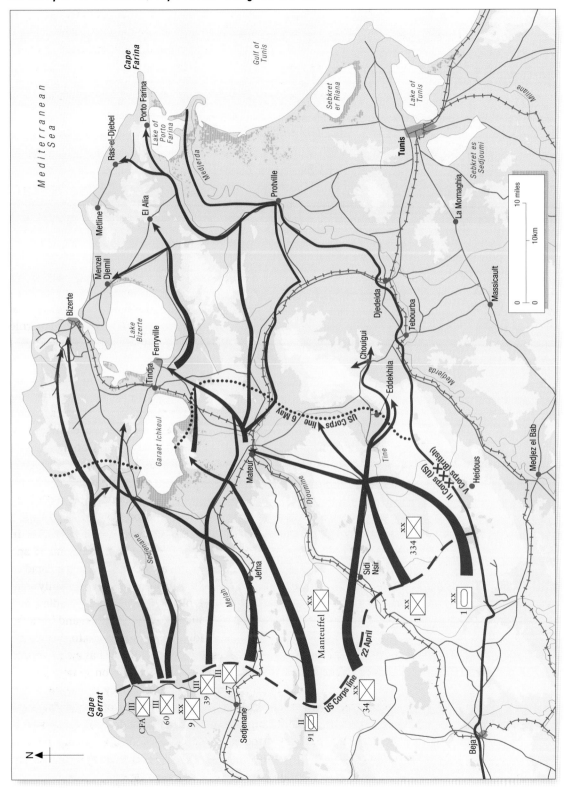

Opposite: Bradley on
board the command ship
USS *Ancon* off the coast of
Sicily on July 8, 1943 at
the start of Operation
Husky. (NARA)

Following the successful
conclusion of the Tunisia
campaign, Patton and
Bradley visited the
training ground of the
82nd Airborne Division
to discuss the upcoming
Sicily invasion with the
divisional commander,
Maj. Gen. Matthew
Ridgway, and his deputy,
Brig. Gen. Maxwell Taylor.
Bradley had led the
formation of the 82nd
Division in 1942, and
Ridgway had succeeded
him in command before it
converted into an airborne
division. (MHI)

II Corps in Tunisia

II Corps entered combat under Patton and Bradley's command in
mid-March 1943 near Maknassy and El Guettar. Bradley was nearly killed
near Sened when his jeep ran over an Italian antitank mine; it did not
detonate and Bradley was spared. The fighting by the 1st Infantry Division
at El Guettar on March 23, 1943 was the first American victory of the war.
In spite of this and subsequent small successes, Alexander was still wary of
the combat effectiveness of the US Army after Kasserine, and planned to
sideline II Corps in the final stages of the Tunisian campaign, relying entirely
on British forces. Patton and Bradley were insulted and upset by the plans,
and Bradley went to Ike's headquarters to protest. He found that Eisenhower
had taken his own admonitions about coalition warfare a bit too completely,
and was oblivious to the lingering damage that Alexander's plans would
have on the reputation of the US Army. Bradley was able to convince
Eisenhower that II Corps could play a useful role by shifting to the northern
sector near Bizerte in order to take part in the final campaign to rid North
Africa of the Axis. Ike agreed, but the experience ignited an ember in Bradley
that remained intense through the war. He remained convinced that
Eisenhower would not necessarily protect American interests in debates
with the British, and he began to see himself as a critical proponent of the
American perspective in inter-Allied decision-making. Patton strongly
agreed with this viewpoint, and it helped bind the two commanders
together in spite of all of their personal differences.

Patton had been assigned to the command of the Seventh US Army for
the invasion of Sicily in the summer of 1943, so he left II Corps under
Bradley's command in mid-April to complete the planning process for
Operation *Husky*. Having been criticized earlier for not imposing his will on
subordinate commanders in the previous fighting, Ike
sent II Corps a relatively detailed set of instructions for
the forthcoming campaign. Bradley found the plans to be
lacking, and he was determined to follow his own best
judgment. Rather than rely on Eisenhower's plan for an
infantry-armor team through the valleys that would be
vulnerable to German control of the heights, Bradley
instead employed the more difficult but rewarding tactics
of an infantry slog along the high ground, culminating
in a vicious and costly assault by the 34th Division on Hill
609. It was one of the epic battles of Tunisia and ended in
a final capture of the crest with tank support in terrain
that seemed impassable to tanks; a German later
complained that the use of the tanks on the plateau had
been "unfair."

The next stage of the campaign in the northern sector
of the front made much more extensive use of armor due
to the favorable ground conditions. The 1st Armored
Division helped spearhead the attack on Bizerte, but it was

still the skillful use of infantry that ensured the eventual capture of the city. Eisenhower was elated by Bradley's performance, and recommended that the popular war correspondent, Ernie Pyle, go and "discover Bradley." Pyle had long been an advocate of "GI Joe" and had never been a big fan of Patton and his "chickenshit" rules and regulations. Sharing Bradley's populist sentiments, Pyle began to celebrate Bradley in his stories, finally bringing him to national attention. It was Pyle who labeled Bradley the "GI General," a characterization that Bradley relished.

Operation *Husky*

The plans for the invasion of Sicily revealed Alexander's continuing contempt for the inexperienced American army. Under the plan, the brunt of the campaign would be undertaken by Montgomery's Eighth Army which was directed to punch up the east coast of the island aside Mount Etna and seize Messina. Patton's Seventh US Army was assigned a largely supporting role as flank guard further to the west. Bradley remained in command of II Corps under Patton. II Corps provided the main landing force in the American sector of Operation *Husky* with the 3rd Division landing at Licata, 1st Division at Gela, and 45th Division at Scoglitti. The Germans followed their doctrine to the letter and countered the landings with a ferocious counterattack consisting of an Italian armored attack from the west and a German attack from further east. The 1st Division at Gela was hard pressed by the assault, but the Allied navies turned in a stunning performance, stopping the Axis tank attack with a crushing barrage of naval gunfire. Operation *Husky* was the first joint Allied amphibious operation against contested shore, and the overall performance of all parties concerned – ground, air, and sea – was exceptionally well conducted. There were some glitches, particularly a disastrous paratroop drop by the 82nd Airborne Division that ran the gantlet of Allied naval gunfire due to some serious command-and-control confusion.

The senior American commanders for Operation *Husky* are seen here (left to right): Ernie Harmon (2nd Armored Division), Manton Eddy (9th Infantry Division), Bradley (II Corps), Charles Ryder (34th Division), Lucian Truscott (3rd Infantry Division), and Hugh Gaffey (Patton's deputy). (NARA)

Bradley was not wildly enamored of Patton's tendency to micromanage operations, particularly his tendency to skirt the usual chain of command and skip II Corps Headquarters to deal directly with divisions under his command. While they had some serious tactical disagreement over prerogatives of command, they generally shared a common operational perspective. The Eighth Army effort towards Catania seemed prudent during the initial planning stages when German forces on the island were scant. But the Germans had reinforced Sicily with some serious units in the weeks

prior to the landing, and they had erected a formidable set of defenses on either side of Mount Etna. Montgomery attempted to redeem the situation by shifting his focus from the stalemate on the Catania plain to the corridor west of Mount Etna, thereby forcing Bradley to cede a critical road network to the British XXX Corps. Patton did not forcibly challenge Montgomery's change, because he had his own ambitions. He convinced Alexander and Eisenhower to permit him to seize the provincial capital of Palermo on the northern coast using a provisional corps created under his deputy commander, Lt. Gen. Geoffrey Keyes. The capture of Palermo was conducted against an ineffectual Italian defense, and helped draw attention to Patton's Seventh US Army at a time when Montgomery's Eighth Army was still bogged down in Etna's foothills.

While Keyes's corps was racing to Palermo and capturing most of western Sicily, Bradley's II Corps faced a tough grind along the British left flank in the mountains west of Etna. The 1st Division fought a particularly grueling battle against German forces near Troina. The Mussolini government was deposed on July 25 prompting Hitler to begin executing a withdrawal operation from

Bradley's II Corps captures Bizerte, May 7, 1943

The culmination of Bradley's II Corps campaign in Tunisia was the capture of the port of Bizerte on May 7, 1943, helping to trap the last of the Axis forces against the coast. This scene shows the advance of Manton Eddy's 9th Division into Bizerte with the support of M3 medium tanks of the 751st Tank Battalion. While the use of tanks for infantry support became commonplace in the later campaigns in Italy and the European theater, at the time of the Tunisian campaign, there were no firm guidelines of doctrine. The US Army in 1940–42 had seen a radical reversal in its tank policy, abandoning its 1918–40 doctrine that tied the tank force to the infantry as a supporting arm. The US Army's lesson from the 1940 Battle of France was that tanks should be consolidated into armored divisions which would be used on their own missions, and primarily used for conducting deep exploitation missions once a breakthrough was won by the infantry. This doctrine was reflected in the US Army order of battle in Tunisia, where most of the tank force was concentrated under 1st Armored Division command. However, Bradley was not convinced that tank–infantry support was unnecessary, and in the early spring of 1943, II Corps began to take steps to reintegrate tanks into the infantry mission by using the handful of separate tank battalions in the theater. Bradley made imaginative use of tank support for the difficult mission of taking Hill 609 in late April 1943. During the final push to the Tunisian coast, Bradley insisted that the infantry receive tank support when possible, especially in urban missions. As a result, the 751st Tank Battalion (Medium) was attached to Eddy's 9th Division for the push into Bizerte. Bradley's successful creation of tank–infantry teams in the later stages of the Tunisian campaign was a precursor of the later pattern of attaching a tank battalion and tank destroyer battalion to each infantry division in the ETO. Bradley's innovations helped to redress the imbalance in US Army armored warfare doctrine at a critical stage of the war. This was part of a broader effort to correct mistaken doctrine and introduce more realistic tactics based on the lessons of the Kasserine defeat.

Sicily to save what he could from the German garrison on Sicily in order to continue the fight on the Italian mainland. The Allies failed to appreciate the withdrawal effort, expecting another fight to the death as had occurred in Tunisia. Once they realized that the Axis forces were evacuating the island, both Patton and Montgomery began desperate, last-minute attempts to race to Messina, including the use of amphibious landings. On the north coast, Patton ordered the 1st, 9th, and 3rd Divisions to converge on Messina along with an amphibious raid by a regimental combat team from the 45th Division. Bradley protested parts of the order to Patton, pointing out that the scheme would result in a collision between 3rd and 45th Division with the risk of ensuing fratricide. Patton shrugged off the complaint, but Bradley was able to work out methods to avoid needless casualties. Much to Patton's delight, the 3rd Division, along with a small contingent from the 45th Division, was the first into the city with a British spearhead arriving an hour later. Patton congratulated the British on "a jolly good race."

Lt. Gen. Omar Bradley in a rare portrait while II Corps commander on Sicily in 1943. Bradley's uniforms were as unadorned as Patton's were flamboyant. (MHI)

Operation *Husky* was both an impressive accomplishment from some perspectives, but a hollow victory in other respects. It precipitated the Italian withdrawal from the war, accomplishing its strategic mission. In addition, it laid the groundwork for joint Allied amphibious operations, a hallmark of future campaigns. On the other hand, the Allied failure to appreciate the German and Italian evacuation across the straits of Messina was a major operational blunder that allowed the Germans to save most of their forces on Sicily, thereby making the Allied landings on the Italian mainland later that autumn all the more difficult.

From a US command perspective, Sicily completely reversed the polarities of senior command. Patton had displayed remarkable political savvy in his

Bradley drives to the 45th Division in Caltanisette on Sicily on July 18, 1943 in his ¾-ton Command and Reconnaissance Truck to discuss the progress of the Sicily campaign. Unlike Patton's command cars, Bradley's vehicles were standard and unadorned. (MHI)

race to Palermo and had once again redeemed the honor of the US Army in the face of lingering British condescension. On the other hand, his schemes were often reckless and at times seemed needlessly self-serving. He was physically and emotionally exhausted by the campaign, and in two separate incidents he slapped shell-shocked soldiers he encountered at field hospitals. Eisenhower attempted to sweep the incidents under the rug, but once they became public back in the United States in the autumn of 1943 Patton's career was in serious jeopardy. Eisenhower's assessment of the senior American commanders began to shift. Patton remained in command of the Seventh US Army for a time, but his career went into limbo for much of late 1943 and early 1944 while he weathered the storm of public protest over the slapping incidents on Sicily. Bradley's performance in Tunisia and Sicily had been textbook examples of solid leadership, and Bradley's cool and professional execution stood in stark contrast to Patton's exuberant and manic style. Eisenhower felt far more comfortable with Bradley's leadership, which fell much more closely into the managerial approach that had become the American art of war under Marshall and the other reformers in the 1930s. Eisenhower reported back to Marshall that of the three commanders, Patton, Clark, and Bradley, "Bradley is the best rounded in all respects, counting experience, and he has the great characteristic of never giving his commander one moment of worry."

Ike decided to shift Bradley over to Fifth US Army as deputy to Mark Clark for the forthcoming Operation *Avalanche* landings at Salerno. Bradley again found himself under the command of a senior leader almost every bit as egotistical and self-centered as Patton, without any of Patton's proven battlefield prowess. Eisenhower viewed Bradley as a potential substitute for Clark should he be transferred to another command, such as leadership of the US troops for the invasion of France in 1944. In late August, Marshall stressed the need to begin preparing for the cross-Channel landings. Eisenhower pushed Clark for the job due to his ample experience in planning amphibious landings, and still having a high opinion of his talents even if not yet displayed on the field of battle. But Marshall felt more confident in Bradley, and Ike concurred.

Bradley departed Europe for the United States in early September to meet with Marshall and to be introduced to President Roosevelt. At the same time, he began creating the future staff for the First US Army, plundering the headquarters from Tunisia and Sicily. His deputy was Courtney Hodges, a dependable officer but one older and more conservative than Bradley. His G-1 was Joseph "Red" O'Hare, a former West Point football teammate who others considered imperious and not especially bright, but who Bradley admired for his common sense and stubbornness. The G-2 slot went to Col. "Monk" Dickson, the former II Corps G-2 who had predicted the Kasserine attack.

Bradley's new command, the First US Army, would contain two corps on D-Day. V Corps was commanded by Leonard "Gee" Gerow, a World War I veteran, a classmate of Bradley's at the 1924 Infantry School course, and a former head of War Plans. Gerow was highly regarded, though he had not seen combat in a senior command slot. The other corps slated to take part in the landings was VII Corps, first headed by Maj. Gen. Roscoe Woodruff. He was a classmate of Bradley's at West Point though not a close friend and he had no combat experience in senior command. Bradley was a bit concerned about the lack of combat experience in the *Overlord* landing team, and he attempted to snag Lucian Truscott who had served so ably as a divisional commander on Sicily. However Truscott's talents were highly prized by Mark Clark and the Fifth US Army, and he remained in Italy for the time being. One of Bradley's more fortuitous discoveries was Maj. Gen. J. Lawton Collins, better known as "Lightning Joe" from his radio call sign when in command of the 25th "Lightning" Division on Guadalcanal. Collins had been brought to the ETO by Ike along with Charles "Cowboy Pete" Corlett to instill a bit of Pacific experience in the green command leadership. Bradley pushed Woodruff aside and installed Collins in the VII Corps command slot while Corlett went to the new XIX Corps.

The senior command for *Overlord* remained in Ike's hands as head of Supreme Headquarters Allied Expeditionary Force (SHAEF). His three deputy commands for land, sea, and air were all British and all trusted commanders from the Mediterranean theater. Bradley had been harshly critical of Ike's performance in the Mediterranean theater, but his viewpoint changed in Britain. Eisenhower had grown in his new command position, and Bradley found that he had become far more confident and self-assured in his abilities in the intervening year. Bradley realized that Ike had to represent the Allied

Command decisions: Patton and Bradley on Sicily, July 1943

During Operation *Husky*, the Allied invasion of Sicily in July–August 1943, Bradley's II Corps was subordinate to Patton's Seventh Army. Here, on July 25, Patton (1) holds an impromptu meeting in an olive grove with Lt. Gen. Omar Bradley (2) and Maj. Gen. Troy Middleton (3) of the 45th Division. By this stage of the campaign, Middleton's division was on the northern coast of Sicily moving towards Messina. The division had taken significant losses during the fighting, suffering 1,156 casualties but capturing 10,977 prisoners. Following the capture of Santo Stefano on July 30, the division was pulled back to prepare for another operation, the landings at Salerno on the Italian mainland. The 3rd Division took its place. Aside from tactical matters, Patton wanted Middleton to dump the cartoonist from the division's mimeographed newspaper, the *Forty-fifth Division News*. Middleton had encouraged the paper as a way to keep the division's enlisted men informed and to kill the numerous rumors that were floating around. One of the young and unknown writers, Bill Mauldin, had begun to add cartoons of two "dogface GI's" named Willie and Joe starting with the second issue. The two soldiers were depicted realistically as unshaven and a bit disheveled, and Patton took offense at the "damned unsoldierly Willie and Joe." Middleton felt that the newspaper served its purpose and shielded Mauldin from Patton's wrath. Mauldin would later go on to become the best-known and most popular army cartoonist of the war, and an award-winning political cartoonist after the war. Bradley stayed out of the controversy, and he found Patton's attitudes towards the common soldier to be excessive and counterproductive.

view in his decision-making, not the American view. Nevertheless, Bradley often pressured Eisenhower to take a more national view on several key operational decisions, in many cases suspecting that Ike had caved into British pressures too easily in order to maintain harmony. Bradley increasingly began to view himself as the main advocate for the American point of view on major operational decisions.

Bradley was not especially happy to learn that Bernard Montgomery had been selected as the *Overlord* land commander. Bradley accepted that Montgomery was Britain's best field commander, but he was tactless and egocentric in a position that required a measure of political acumen. Aside from the obvious lack of chemistry between Bradley and Montgomery, there were fundamental differences in viewpoints on the art-of-war. Montgomery had developed a tactical style, sometimes dubbed "colossal cracks," which focused on the need for methodical planning and preparation. Montgomery's approach struck Bradley as too reminiscent of the style of methodical battle developed in the final phases of World War I that did not take sufficient account of the changes in the offensive–defensive balance and the change in tempo made possible by the use of combined-arms warfare and tanks. Bradley believed that modern warfare required a greater willingness to deal with the inherent uncertainties of the battlefield by being willing to improvise and adapt to new circumstances. When Montgomery's post-D-Day plans were shown to Bradley, he insisted on deleting the phase lines outlining the pace of operations in the American sector.

Bradley had little to do with the overall *Overlord* planning, which was well underway by the time that he arrived in Britain. Both Montgomery and Eisenhower were concerned that the original invasion force was too weak, and steps were underway to increase the force to five divisions: two British, one Canadian, and two American. Bradley recommended a night landing instead of a daytime landing, but he was promptly overruled by both British and American planners who were intimidated by the execution of such a complex operation in the din and confusion of night time. Although the original plan included some airborne forces, Bradley pressed for a maximum commitment of two airborne divisions in the American sector which were intended to create a deep shoulder on the right flank of Utah Beach. Bradley continued to urge this option in spite of opposition from various quarters. Admittedly, the airborne landings on Sicily had been a mess, but Bradley argued that the lessons had been learned. The Normandy air boss, RAF Air Chief Marshal Trafford Leigh-Mallory, took a very pessimistic view of likely airborne casualties, but Bradley prevailed.

The senior command of the Seventh US Army at the headquarters in Palermo after the fighting: II Corps commander Lt. Gen. Omar Bradley, Seventh Army commander Lt. Gen. George Patton, and Patton's deputy, Maj. Gen. Geoffrey Keyes. Keyes was in charge of the special corps that Patton created to make the lightning advance on Palermo during the campaign. (MHI)

Bradley's D-Day forces consisted of Collins' VII Corps to the right on Utah Beach, spearheaded by the 4th Division, and Gerow's V Corps on Omaha Beach, spearheaded by regimental combat teams from the 1st and 29th Divisions. Bradley boarded the cruiser USS *Augusta* in a bad mood. He had developed a boil on his nose that was serious enough that it had to be lanced by a naval corpsman. Bradley was not the handsomest of men in the best of times, and a prominent bandage now marred his visage. Although not especially vain, the few photos of Bradley from this important moment were taken after D-Day once Bradley had the bandage removed. Bradley was cooped up on the cruiser *Augusta* when the D-Day actions began on the night of June 5–6.

Ike, Winston Churchill, and Bradley enjoy an impromptu shooting match with the new M1 .30-cal. carbine during a visit to the 2nd Armored Division in 1944. (MHI)

The airborne landings on the night of June 5–6 were a glorious shambles. Both the 82nd and 101st Airborne Divisions were scattered all over the Cotentin Peninsula and few units captured their objectives on time. Nevertheless, both divisions were blessed by a deep reservoir of self-motivated young warriors who set out as best they could to carry out their missions deep behind German lines. As a result, Germans defenses behind Utah Beach began to disintegrate in confusion and chaos. Senior German commanders were convinced that the dispersion was a maniacal new form of chaotic warfare designed to capitalize on the virtues of self-contained elite commandos. Bradley was largely unaware of the course of these actions until late in the day due to the usual command-and-control problems with the paratroop radio network.

The landings by the 4th Division at Utah Beach proceeded like clockwork except that the spearhead regimental combat team landed a distance away from the intended sector. This was all for the better as the landing sector included a much weaker German strongpoint than the planned beachhead, and this particular strongpoint had been neutralized by the pre-invasion bombardment. The 4th Division was off the beach and moving across the flooded farm fields by late morning.

Omaha Beach was a disaster. There was a serious misunderstanding between Bradley's First US Army and the Eighth Air Force heavy bomber force. Bradley was under the impression that the heavy bombers would bomb parallel to the beach and saturate the defenses, not only knocking out much of the defensive fieldworks, but also cratering the beach to give the landing troops some cover. The US Army Air Force received conflicting demands from the Army, some elements wanting a cratered beach and others wanting the use of small bombs to avoid cratering since the beach would be needed for logistics purposes in the follow-on waves. Furthermore, the Omaha Beach area had an extensive array of radar-directed Flak.

As a result, the USAAF decided to conduct the attack perpendicular to the beach to minimize the vulnerability of the bombers to Flak. The resulting bombardment was a complete waste. The early morning cloud cover interfered with aiming, and rather than risks the horrors of fratricide against the crowded transport ships, the bombers dropped their payloads 30 seconds late, churning up farm fields deep behind the beach, but leaving the German defenses intact. The Allied naval bombardment was inadequate to suppress the defenses at Omaha Beach due to timing issues related the vagaries of the tidal flows on the several Normandy landing beaches.

In spite of the shortcomings of the bombardment, the real problem was the nature of the German defenses at Omaha Beach. Omaha Beach was a narrow beach overlooked by high bluffs. The only way off the beach was through three ravines, called "draws" by the US Army. The Germans fully appreciated the advantages of these ravines and created a strongpoint at each of these exits. Not only were the three draws heavily fortified, but Omaha Beach had an unusually dense concentration of German infantry forces. Rommel had visited the Grandcamps sector in February and saw an uncanny resemblance between the future Omaha Beach and the landing site at Salerno which he had visited a few months before. He uttered the ominous judgment that "the fate of Europe will be decided here" and ordered his staff to deploy a regular infantry division, the 352. Infanterie-Division to this sector on top of the existing static division already in place. One of its regiments was added to the Omaha Beach defenses unnoticed by Allied intelligence. Most of its divisional artillery was within range of the beach, with the landing sites in front of the draws already prepared as pre-registered kill-zones. Allied intelligence thought that the 352. Infanterie-Division was deep behind the beach around Saint-Lô and had no idea that the Germans planned to defend the beach so vigorously.

At the heart of the Omaha Beach debacle was a serious Allied misperception of German tactical intentions. German doctrine did not favor a vigorous defense of the beachhead but preferred a weak forward defense followed by a violent counterattack. This had been the pattern on Sicily and at Salerno and Anzio, and the US Army expected the same at Omaha Beach: a relatively easy landing that would have to be quickly reinforced before facing a strong German counterattack. Unfortunately, Rommel's assessment of the lessons of the Italian fighting convinced him that German doctrine regarding amphibious landings was bankrupt and he tried to change it by stressing the need for stiff defense on the beachhead itself. Omaha Beach was the only Allied landing site where this was fully carried out. There was a shortage of regular

Bradley's deputy during his command of the First US Army was Maj. Gen. Courtney Hodges, who then took over command of the army in August 1944 when Bradley was elevated to 12th Army Group command. (MHI)

infantry divisions and the only other one in lower Normandy was near Dieppe where Rommel also felt an Allied landing would be likely. The rest of the German divisions were third-rate static units. Omaha Beach had double the infantry and double or triple the machine guns, antitank guns, and field guns of any of the D-Day beaches.

The initial landings on Omaha Beach aimed straight into the two strongest German strongpoints at Colleville and Vierville, and not surprisingly, faced a horrific firestorm of small arms, mortars, and field guns. It was far closer in intensity to a World War I battlefield. On the east side at the Colleville draw, the experienced 16th Infantry, 1st Division, took serious casualties, but its young NCOs and junior officers quickly and efficiently began leading small parties off the beach and up over the bluffs. The green 116th Infantry of the 29th Division took appalling casualties and was slower to move off the beach. The follow-on waves were stymied by large sections of anticraft obstacles still lurking in the waters off the beach that engineers had failed to clear due to their decimation in the early waves. Young navy and coast guard captains finally ignored the obstacles and headed to shore anyway. By late morning, a steady stream of LCIs (Landing Craft Infantry) were shuttling back and forth from the transports off-shore to the beach.

Bradley was out of touch with the beach for much of the morning due to the usual problems with radios becoming damaged in the surf. The reports from navy officers near the shore were discouraging. Bradley contemplated grim options including abandoning the beach and shifting V Corps to either neighboring British beaches or to Utah Beach. In the event, he gritted his teeth and waited for the junior commanders to sort things out ashore. By afternoon, it was clear that V Corps was firmly ashore at Omaha Beach even if casualties had been painfully high.

The much-anticipated German counterattack never materialized at either Utah or Omaha Beaches. The 352. Infanterie-Division tried to stage several company-size attacks on the afternoon and evening of D-Day, but they were broken by naval gunfire or infantry defenses. The division's mobile battlegroup had been prematurely committed early on D-Day morning to chase down the phantom paratroopers, and spent most of the day wandering about the Normandy countryside obeying orders and counterorders, all the while under intense Allied counterattack.

Into the bocage

On June 12, a delegation of all the senior American commanders including Gen. George C. Marshall, Adm. Ernest King and Gen. Hap Arnorld

Bradley spent several days after D-Day touring the battlefront with senior Allied commanders. He is seen here on June 15 in a LCVP off the coast with Rear Admiral Alan Kirk who commanded the US Navy contingent on D-Day. (MHI)

accompanied Ike and Bradley on a tour of the Normandy sector. In spite of the high costs suffered at Omaha Beach, the landings had gone exceptionally well and the Allies were firmly ashore in France.

Bradley's immediate task in the week after D-Day was to link up Omaha and Utah Beaches. A Ranger force had been delivered against the Pointe-du-Hoc gun emplacements between the two beaches, so for the next two days, forces from Omaha Beach began to push to the west to link up with the Rangers. In the neighboring VII Corps sector near Utah Beach, Bradley intended to consolidate the scattered airborne divisions and then to direct VII Corps to a rapid assault on Cherbourg. By D+3 the focus was changed again; in both sectors, the US troops were facing an unexpected hindrance, the bocage. The farm fields in this section of lower Normandy were bordered by thick hedgerows to shield the crops from the coastal winds. These hedgerows created a form of natural fortification that the Germans began to exploit to slow the pace of the American advance out of the beachheads. The slow advance in the bocage convinced both Bradley and Collins that a quick capture of Cherbourg was unlikely. Under these circumstances, it became imperative to cut off the Cotentin Peninsula from any further German reinforcements. The first issue was completing the link-up of the elements of the 82nd Airborne Division on either side of the Mederet River. Once this was accomplished, Collins moved the newly arrived 90th Division forward to take over the task of moving westward by June 10. The 90th was another division based on National Guard troops and its performance proved to be exceptionally poor. Bradley agreed to pull the unit out of the line and substitute it with the experienced 9th Infantry Division, which accomplished the mission by June 17. The neighboring V Corps continued its slow grind into the bocage, aiming for the road junction at Saint-Lô.

On June 18, 1944, Field Marshal Bernard Montgomery laid out the immediate tasks for the Allied forces in Normandy. The First US Army was assigned to take Cherbourg while the British Second Army was to take Caen. The main assault on Cherbourg began on the evening of June 19. The initial attacks made steady progress as the German units tended to withdraw after first contact. By June 20, VIII Corps had reached the Cap de la Hague Peninsula and encountered the German main line of resistance. The final attack on Cherbourg on June 22 was preceded by an intense air preparation conducted by IX Tactical Air Command. By June 24, the German defenses began to crumble and breaches were made in the final layer of outer fortifications, providing access to the city itself. Infantry began assaulting Fort de Roule overlooking the city and, on June 26, US intelligence learned that the German command bunker was located in the

The principal American commanders have a group portrait taken after D-Day. Left to right are Bradley (FUSA); Leonard "Gee" Gerow (V Corps – Omaha Beach), Eisenhower (SHAEF) and J. Lawton "Lightning Joe" Collins (VII Corps – Utah Beach). (MHI)

Saint-Saveur neighborhood. The tunnel entrance of the bunker was assaulted, and the command staff of Festung Cherbourg surrendered. Two more days were spent eliminating outlying forts in the harbor, mainly by air attack and tank gunfire; a total of 6,000 prisoners were captured. On July 1, Collins reported that all organized resistance on the Cotentin Peninsula had ended. The allies had hoped to capture Cherbourg by D+15, so its liberation on D+21 was not far behind schedule, especially compared to the plans for Caen in the neighboring British sector. The capture of Cherbourg did not provide any immediate benefit to the Allied supply situation, as the Germans had thoroughly demolished the port facilities prior to the surrender. It took almost two months to clean up the port, and it was only back in operation by September 1944. Cherbourg was the first major Allied victory following the D-Day landings.

With Cherbourg in Allied hands, Bradley refocused the direction of the First US Army attack towards Saint-Lô with an aim to push out of the constraints of the bocage country and into more open ground to the south. On July 3, Bradley launched a five-division attack by Eddy's VIII Corps and Collins' VII Corps towards Coutances. The attack made little progress and Bradley was forced to reinforce it with Corlett's XIX Corps on July 7. The 117th Infantry, 30th Division, executed a textbook crossing of the Vire River, and Bradley reinforced the success with a combat command from the 3rd Armored Division. The threat along the Vire River prompted the Germans to shift the Panzer-Lehr-Division from the British sector to deal with the slow but steady American advance. The Panzers attacked near La Desert and were badly smashed up, but they put a temporary halt to Bradley's offensive.

Even if the attack in the bocage had stalled again, Bradley was becoming more confident that a breakout was becoming more likely. In late June, the SHAEF developed a plan called *Lucky Strike* to create a breakout if any sector of German defensive line in Normandy began to crack. Bradley was convinced that the Germans had committed most of their reserves and that they lacked any defense in depth in his sector. His revised version of the *Lucky Strike* plan was dubbed Operation *Cobra*. After winning Eisenhower's approval, he outlined the *Cobra* plan to the corps commanders and senior staff at his Omaha Beach headquarters on July 12. The original plan expected to start the operation on 18 July, but this proved premature as the vital city of Saint-Lô was not firmly in US hands until 19 July and the Periers–Saint-Lô road was not secured until July 20. The strategic bomber force had been redirected to supporting Montgomery's Operation *Goodwood* in the meantime, delaying the attack a few more days.

Cooperation with the USAAF tactical air forces was vital to the American success in Operation *Cobra*, and here Bradley and his chief-of-staff William Kean are seen talking with the commander of the 9th Tactical Air Command, Maj. Gen. Elwood "Pete" Quesada. (NARA)

Ike and Bradley visit Maj. Gen. Ira Wyche, commander of the 79th Division, at his field command post near Haunville, France on July 4, 1944. (MHI)

The *Cobra* plan was finalized in field orders on July 20. *Cobra* took on added importance when Operation *Goodwood* failed to achieve a breakthrough in the British sector. At a cost of more than a third of the total British tank strength in theater, the offensive had captured only 32 square miles of territory and made a penetration barely 6 miles deep. In spite of these disappointing results, *Goodwood* had vital consequences for Operation *Cobra* since it reinforced the German belief that the main Allied thrust would come in the British sector. As a result, German units in Bradley's sector remained starved of new Panzer forces.

Bradley proposed to launch the ground offensive in the immediate aftermath of a carpet-bombing attack, with the US troops only 800 yards from the edge of the bomb zone. As at Omaha Beach, there was some serious miscommunication between the ground and air commanders. Bradley expected that the bombers would attack parallel to the Periers–Saint-Lô road, providing a natural and visible boundary for the northern side of the kill-zone. Once again, the USAAF decided to attack perpendicular to the road.

Glider assault on Normandy, June 6, 1944

Bradley had helped to reactivate the 82nd Division in 1942, though it remained a conventional infantry division until after Maj. Gen. Matthew Ridgway took command when it was converted to an airborne division. Bradley was an enthusiastic proponent of airborne operations even after their inauspicious debut in Operation *Husky*, where Allied ships shot up a glider relief mission. During the planning phase for Operation *Overlord*, Bradley was one of the principal advocates for the use of both US Army airborne divisions to reinforce the attack at Utah Beach. The airborne divisions had a triangular structure with two parachute infantry regiments and one glider infantry regiment. The first glider landings were conducted in the early morning hours of June 6, with the 101st Airborne Division's Mission *Chicago* involving 52 gliders landing in the dark at 0325hrs, followed shortly by the 82nd Airborne Division's Mission *Detroit* involving 46 gliders landing around 0410hrs. The initial drops were conducted using C-47 transport aircraft as tugs and Waco CG-4A gliders. They were followed in the late evening of D-Day by two resupply missions, *Keokuk* and *Elmira*, which landed around 2100hrs. Two more resupply missions were flown on the morning of D+1, landing around 0700hrs. The use of gliders in airborne assaults was still immature and there were large numbers of casualties because of crashes and premature releases over the ocean; some 123 troops were casualties in the Waco gliders and 340 in the larger Horsa gliders. Gliders were an important adjunct to paratroopers since they could be used to bring in larger items such as jeeps and artillery and were more practical for supply missions. During D-Day glider missions by the two US divisions, a total of 95 pack howitzers and antitank guns were delivered as well as 290 vehicles and 238 tons of supplies.

Bradley greets Walter Bedell "Beetle" Smith. Beetle had been one of Bradley's protégés at the Infantry School in the 1930s and served as Eisenhower's deputy in 1944–45. He was a tough and hard-nosed administrator, with a dyspeptic temperament propelled by ulcers, cigarettes, and dexedrine, with all "the natural charm of a rattlesnake" according to his contemporaries. (NARA)

Operation *Cobra* was scheduled to begin at 1300hrs on July 24, 1944, after the heavy bomber attack. The bomber mission was cancelled late in the morning due to heavy overcast but the halt message arrived after the heavy bombers were already airborne. Some bombers continued the mission unaware of the cancellation and the lead bombardier of one unit accidentally released his payload prematurely, followed by the 15 other aircraft of his formation. These fell 2,000 yards north of the bomb zone, killing 25 and wounding 131 soldiers of the 30th Division. A series of heated discussions between Bradley and the USAAF commanders ensued.

Operation *Cobra* was rescheduled for the morning of July 25 starting with strafing attacks by fighter bombers and followed by a carpet bombing attack by 1,495 B-17s and B-24 heavy bombers and 380 B-26 medium bombers in several waves, dropping 4,700 tons of bombs into an area 7,000 yards long and 2,500 yards wide. The effect on the German defenses was devastating. Of the 3,600 troops under Panzer-Lehr-Division's immediate control, about 1,000 were killed in the bombing attack, and at least as many wounded or severely dazed. The July 25 air attack repeated the problems of the previous day, with bombs again falling short into American lines, killing 111 and wounding 490 soldiers. Among them was Lt. Gen. Lesley McNair, head of Army Ground Forces, the highest ranking US officer to die in the war. The casualties were especially severe in the forward assault companies, causing significant problems in launching the initial attacks.

In spite of the bombing errors, the ground attack began at 1100hrs. The western portion of the attack bogged down quickly and the first day's attack was disappointing. Instead of gaining 3 miles, Collins' VII Corps had only penetrated about a mile. The option was to continue the infantry attack for the next few days in hopes of securing a clean penetration, or act more boldly and commit the mechanized forces the next day. Collins decided on the bolder option. This was based on his assessment that the German defenses were in a shambles. Previously, when US forces in Normandy advanced as far as a mile into German positions, they would inevitably be met with fierce, coordinated counterattacks. Instead, there was very little evidence of any coordinated response. The armored attacks made deep inroads into the German defenses and traffic jams proved to be the main hindrance to the advance on the first day. Bradley directed Collins to take the main objective at Coutances, and in the process, several German divisions were trapped in a series of pockets. By the end of July, the First US Army had captured about 20,000 German troops and had effectively demolished the two German corps and most of their constituent divisions.

Breakout from Normandy, August 1–13, 1944

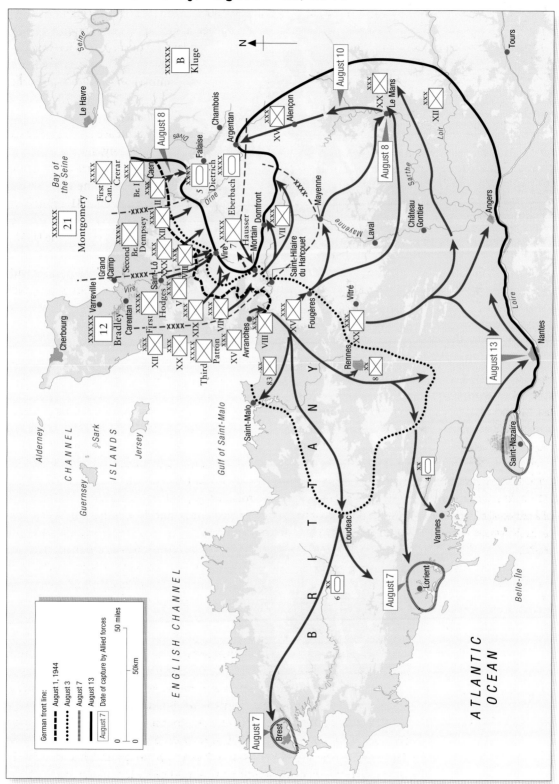

To turn the breakout into a breakthrough, Bradley's secret weapon was Patton. The Third US Army had been secretly moved into the Normandy bridgehead in July with an aim to providing a knockout punch during Operation *Cobra*. The mission of Patton's Third US Army was to push westward into Brittany to seize the ports of Quiberon Bay and Brest. Spearheaded by the green but well-trained 4th and 6th Armored Divisions, Patton's forces were racing into Brittany by the first week of August with negligible German defenses in their way. The addition of Patton's Third US Army also changed the organizational structure of Allied forces in France as well as Bradley's command. With both First and Third US Armies in the field, the 12th Army Group headquarters was inaugurated under Bradley's command, and US forces were divested from Montgomery's 21st Army Group. Bradley took command of the 12th Army Group while his deputy, Courtney Hodges, took over command of the First US Army.

The Brittany operation was remarkable for its speed. The 6th Armored Division reached Brest on August 8, the fastest and deepest operation ever conducted by a single US division in Europe in 1944–45. Yet the strategic goal of seizing the Breton ports was not achieved in full since the armored units were not strong enough to force their way into the fortified ports. Brest did not fall until 19 September and its harbor was completely demolished; plans to assault Lorient and Saint-Nazaire were cancelled and the isolated garrisons did not surrender until the end of the war. While the Breton ports had seemed valuable in July, by August more alluring opportunities had presented themselves.

The 4th Armored Division commander, John Wood, argued with Patton that Brittany was best left to the infantry and that the armored divisions should turn east and head for the Seine River and a deep envelopment of the German Army in Normandy. Patton quickly warmed to this idea and began pushing Bradley in this direction. Bradley had begun to recognize that the original mission in Brittany was far less valuable than originally planned if the Germans again demolished the ports, and intelligence made it clear that the Germans had no means to defend the Seine. A deep encirclement of German forces along the Seine River now seemed a real possibility, which might put better ports such as Le Havre and Antwerp in Allied hands.

Bradley convinced Eisenhower and Montgomery to alter the original *Overlord* plans. The aim shifted from the seizure of the Breton ports to the destruction of the German Army west of the Orne River. These plans became formal on August 3 when Bradley instructed Patton to minimize the forces being used to clear Brittany. Montgomery strongly backed this venture, recognizing that

Following Patton's arrival in France as head of the new Third US Army, he met with Bradley and Montgomery on July 7, 1944 to discuss the forthcoming campaign. (MHI)

it could lead to the Allied right flank sweeping eastward all the way to Paris. Patton's Third US Army was directed along the axis of Laval–Le Mans–Chartres with only a single corps left behind in Brittany. During the midst of this change in direction, the Germans struck with Operation *Lüttich*.

Hitler was deeply alarmed by the rapid American progress out of the Saint-Lô area, and ordered a Panzer counteroffensive from the Mortain area towards Avranches to cut off Patton's spearheads. This rash decision depended on the use of Panzer forces that had succeeded in stalemating Montgomery's

Bradley consults with VIII Corps commander, Maj. Gen. Troy Middleton, during the fighting near the port of Saint-Malo on August 16, 1944. (MHI)

21st Army Group near Caen for nearly two months. The redeployment of the badly depleted Panzer forces from the British/Canadian sector over to the American one was an invitation to disaster. Not only did it fundamentally shift the balance in the Caen sector in favor of Montgomery, but it exposed the moving Panzer columns to the predatory attacks of Allied fighter-bombers. Ultra signals intelligence revealed the Mortain attacks, and when the attack began on August 7 US forces had been alerted. The attack bogged down immediately in the face of firm US infantry resistance and the German columns were pummeled by artillery and air attacks. A day later, on the morning of August 8, 1944, the First Canadian Army launched Operation *Totalize*, an offensive aimed at Falaise, 21 miles south of Caen. Against weakened defenses, the Canadian and Polish tanks made steady inroads into the previously impregnable Germans defenses. By the evening of August 10, the German situation had become desperate.

While Eisenhower was at Bradley's field headquarters on August 8, he telephoned Montgomery to suggest a change in US plans. Instead of moving east towards the Seine, the focus of Patton's Third Army would shift north towards Alençon and then to the boundary of the 21st Army Group – roughly along the line from Carrouges to Sees. At this point, if conditions warranted it, Patton's forces could continue their advance across the inter-army boundary towards Argentan. Montgomery was enthusiastic about the potential for such an operation. Although agreeing with the objectives suggested by Bradley, he suspected that the Germans would concentrate their efforts in the bocage country near Alençon where it would be easier to conduct defensive operations. As a result, he pressed the Canadians to pursue their drive on Falaise as rapidly as possible, expecting that they could reach Argentan quicker than the Americans. After this conference, Bradley passed instructions to Patton, and also redirected Hodges' First Army. Instead of moving to the east, First US Army was to overcome the German forces around Mortain, and, using Mortain as a hinge, move northward through Barenton and Domfront toward Flers. The misguided Panzer counterattack at Mortain had left the Wehrmacht

The two American army group commanders in the ETO were Jacob Devers (6th Army Group) to the left and Bradley (12th Army Group) to the right. Between them is Leonard "Gee" Gerow, who headed Army War Plans at the start of the war and led V Corps at Omaha Beach. Devers was outside Eisenhower and Bradley's circle of Mediterranean Theater veterans and commanded the US Army ETO in Britain in 1943 prior to Eisenhower's appointment. (NARA)

vulnerable to a double envelopment in Normandy.

August 13 was a turning point in the final Normandy battles. On the afternoon of August 13, Bradley ordered Haislip to halt any further advance towards the Canadians and to prepare to shift his advance back eastward towards the Seine. Bradley regarded the Falaise operation as being a hammer and anvil, with Montgomery's 21st Army Group playing the hammer role. With the American anvil already in place, Bradley turned his attention to deeper objectives. This decision has been the subject of enormous debate since then, as some critics argue that XV Corps could have sealed the Falaise pocket sooner, thereby capturing more German troops than were bagged when the pocket finally closed a week later on August 20.

Bradley's reasons for the change were straightforward. Patton's troops were already north of the inter-army boundary which had been allotted to the British 21st Army Group. Bradley was concerned that a head-on juncture of the American and Canadian forces would lead to serious fratricide problems, and complicate air support missions. Even though Patton's XV Corps had seized Argentan without heavy loss, their position was far from secure. Bradley preferred a "solid shoulder at Argentan than a broken neck at Falaise." XV Corps had its neck stuck out without secure flanks. To the west, German forces were on the verge of launching another Panzer counterattack designed specifically to cut off the armored spearhead at Argentan, and there was a 20-mile gap separating XV Corps and the advancing elements of the US First Army further west. Bradley's decision was also based on incorrect intelligence that the Germans were already moving the bulk of their forces out of the Falaise pocket. The Allied commanders found it hard to believe that the Germans would be stupid enough to allow the bulk of their forces to be trapped. Bradley instead aimed to eliminate the remaining German forces by a deeper envelopment on the Seine.

By mid-August, the German situation went from bad to catastrophic. On August 15, the Seventh US Army launched Operation *Dragoon* on the Mediterranean coast of France. The two German field armies in central and southern France had been bled to reinforce Normandy, but now faced an unexpected fight of their own. The Germans began to realize that the strategic aim of Operation *Dragoon* was to meet up with Allied forces in central France, essentially trapping Heeresgruppe G in southern and central France. By the second week of August, not only was the Seventh Army in Normandy on the brink of destruction, but the entire German occupation of France was threatened.

On August 16, Canadian forces entered Falaise, nearly closing the trap on the bulk of German units in Normandy. That day Montgomery telephoned Bradley and suggested that the Allied forces link up to the northeast of Argentan, with the Canadian and Polish forces seizing Trun and the Americans taking Chambois. By this time, XV Corps in the Argentan region had been reduced to a holding force with two of its divisions advancing quickly to the east. Late on August 16, Hitler finally consented to a withdrawal order for units trapped in the Falaise pocket. At the time, the German forces in the pocket consisted of the remnants of nine infantry and six Panzer divisions in a killing-zone only 15 miles across, vulnerable to artillery fire from all sides. The last organized groups escaped over the Dives River in the early morning hours of August 21, and by the afternoon, the Falaise pocket was firmly sealed. German units began to surrender en masse to avoid the incessant artillery fire.

Allied forces captured over 50,000 soldiers in the Falaise pocket and over 10,000 were found dead; a total of 313 tanks and assault guns were lost. Estimates of German troops escaping the pocket run from 20,000 to 40,000 troops. The most valuable German units had been shattered beyond recognition. Six of the Panzer divisions that escaped reported to Berlin that they totaled only 2,000 men, 62 tanks, and 26 artillery pieces, less than a tenth of their strength at the outset of the campaign. Nor was their ordeal over. Having escaped the Falaise cauldron, they now would have to run the gauntlet again to escape over the Seine River.

While the Falaise pocket was being sealed, Patton had continued to race eastward towards the Seine against little more than improvised battlegroups. Bradley was still keen to use airborne forces to accelerate the advance, and initial planning began for Operation *Transfigure* on August 17 to trap retreating elements of the German Seventh Army south of Paris and to facilitate Patton's advance. By August 16th, Patton's tanks had almost reached Rambouillet and so the airborne landings were postponed. They were next targeted at seizing bridgeheads over the Seine. Once again, Patton's tank columns were faster, arriving on August 19 near Mantes. By the time that the Falaise pocket was sealed on August 20, Haislip's XV Corps had two divisions on the Seine near Mantes above Paris and already had begun crossing the river on August 19.

On August 19, Eisenhower met with Montgomery and Bradley to discuss operational planning. The original D-Day plans had not expected Allied forces to reach the outer boundary of the D-Day lodgment area until D+90, when in fact it had been reached on D+74. All three commanders agreed to ignore earlier plans and to exploit the current German predicament. Bradley broached the problem posed by Haislip's intrusion into the British 21st Army Group sector near Mantes.

Bradley and Patton share a ride in a C-47 transport aircraft on an inspection of the Brittany front on August 31, 1944. By this stage of the campaign, Patton's forces in Brittany had been reduced to a single corps to enable him to shift his resources to the Seine River on the approaches to Paris. (NARA)

Bradley offered to provide Montgomery with trucks to substitute British forces at Mantes, but Montgomery declined due to his focus on the Falaise operation. Montgomery had long been a proponent of a long envelopment on the Seine, which might trap as many as 75,000 German troops on the left bank. As a result, Montgomery encouraged Bradley to ignore the inter-Allied boundaries and exploit the opportunity.

By August 24, Patton's forces had crossed the Seine both north and south of Paris. While it might seem that Paris would have fallen under the purview of Patton's Third Army, on 23 August, Bradley substantially reconfigured the 12th Army Group composition to disentangle the eastward drive. Haislip's XV Corps was shifted to First US Army control; Patton's Third US Army continued its rapid advance eastward over the Seine with its focus to the south of the city. The primary constraint to all of these operations was the lack of fuel, and the 12th Army Group was forced to develop improvised means to supply the advance columns, such as the Red Ball Express truck columns and an airlift of fuel to captured airbases immediately behind the front lines.

On August 19, a revolt had broken out in Paris led by the French resistance. Allied planning had not seriously considered Paris as an objective. Bradley later remarked that "Tactically, the city had become meaningless. For all its past glories, Paris represented nothing more than an inkspot on our maps to be bypassed as we headed toward the Rhine. Logistically it could cause untold trouble, for behind its handsome facades there lived 4,000,000 hungry Frenchmen." Bradley's staff had estimated that Paris would require 4,000 tons of supplies per day, which was equivalent to the amount needed to push Patton's Third US Army three days closer towards the German border. During a meeting on August 22, Bradley and Eisenhower agreed that the situation in Paris was getting out of hand and that they would have to intervene regardless of previous planning. Eisenhower had already promised that Leclerc's 2e Division Blindée would be given the honor, but Bradley wanted it reinforced with American troops, given Leclerc's penchant for independent action. The 2e Division Blindée and the 4th Infantry Division penetrated into the city on August 24, and the weak German garrison quickly collapsed.

The last two weeks of August 1944 saw the total collapse of the Wehrmacht in France. While some areas remained in German control – the Saar, Lorraine, Alsace – most of France was liberated. The Wehrmacht lost some 300,000 troops killed and captured plus a further 200,000 stranded in the *Festung* ports by Hitler's standfast orders. Nor was the catastrophe yet over. The rapid and deep penetration of Allied armies led to further encirclements in Belgium in early September 1944. The First US Army pushed into Belgium, encircling German troops around Mons. Montgomery's 21st Army Group pushed up alongside and seized the vital port of Antwerp on the run. In the euphoria of the moment, the approach route to the port via the Scheldt Estuary was ignored, one of the major Allied blunders of an otherwise spectacular late summer advance. Patton's Third US Army raced into Lorraine, securing a crossing of the Moselle near Nancy, but acquiring only a toehold on the approaches to Metz due to the heavy fortification in the area. Dever's 6th Army Group had enjoyed an even more spectacular advance from the Mediterranean, reaching Alsace in a lightning advance, and meeting up with Patton's forces on September 10–12, creating a solid front from the North Sea to the Mediterranean.

Autumn frustrations

By the middle of September, the Allied armies were running out of fuel. The explosive advances of late August and early September had pushed them far beyond the wildest expectations of the *Overlord* planners. On September 11, 1944, the first day Bradley's troops entered Germany near Aachen, the Allies were along a phase line that the Operation *Overlord* plans did not expect to reach until D+330, May 2, 1945, some 233 days ahead of schedule. The shortage of fuel led to acrimonious debates about priorities and allotments. Montgomery surprised Eisenhower by offering a bold plan to seize a Rhine River crossing in the Netherlands at Arnhem by a combined paratroop-mechanized operation codenamed *Market-Garden*. Eisenhower's support for this plan inevitably meant that operations by Bradley's 12th Army Group would be curtailed, just as it had reached the German frontier in the First US Army sector. Patton's Third US Army continued its push in Lorraine based largely on captured fuel stocks, but it ground to a halt later in the month after enduring a slapdash counterattack by 5. Panzerarmee. On September 22, Ike issued an order to restrict major combat operations until the supply situation improved. The lull lasted through early November 1944, although some high priority operations did continue on a limited scale, such as the clearing of the Scheldt and the capture of Aachen.

In early September 1944, it seemed as though the German Army was on the verge of a collapse as severe as that which had ended the Kaiser's army in November 1918. But by mid-September, it appeared that the days of "the Void" were coming to an end. German morale improved once the troops were defending German soil, and the Wehrmacht proved remarkably adept at cobbling together a new force of infantry divisions to man the new defensive lines of the West-Stellung. The massive influx of fresh infantry had come from an unlikely source – the Luftwaffe and Kriegsmarine. The Allied bombing campaign against German fuel supplies that had begun in May 1944 had been so effective that the German surface fleet was kept in port and many Luftwaffe units were grounded. The rout of late August and early September had been an aberration, and the Wehrmacht again began to display its usual ferocious defensive prowess.

Bradley's 12th Army Group received a new addition in the early fall, the Ninth

Bradley accompanies Eisenhower on a tour of the front on November 9, 1944, visiting with Lt. Gen. "Gee" Gerow, commander of V Corps (left), and Maj. Gen. Louis Craig, commander of the 9th Infantry Division (right). (NARA)

US Army under Lt. Gen. William Simpson. At first, Bradley planned to insert the Ninth US Army into the Ardennes opposite the Eifel region of Germany. He eventually changed this plan for several reasons. To begin with, Montgomery's Second British Army was a wasting asset due to severe shortages of infantry. The British were already cannibalizing units to maintain battalion strengths, and the situation was unlikely to get better. Bradley was concerned that Montgomery would convince Ike to shed US units to the 21st Army Group, and he preferred that the green Ninth US Army be pilfered rather than the First US Army, the core element of 12th Army Group. Secondly, the failure of Operation *Market-Garden* pushed the Allies further north than originally anticipated, and the First Canadian Army could not hold a long section of the front since in October it had been given the mission of clearing the Scheldt Estuary to open up the port of Antwerp. As a result, Simpson's Ninth US Army was positioned between Montgomery's 21st Army Group and Hodge's First US Army. Control of the Ninth US Army would be a source of continual bickering between Montgomery, Ike, and Bradley.

Bradley's principal preoccupation in late September and early October was the Aachen–Stolberg corridor. The assault of Aachen lasted two weeks from October 10 to 25. The principal objective in the autumn campaign was to reach the Roer River as a precondition for a lunge for the Rhine sometime in early 1945. The campaign was hampered by lingering supply shortages, abnormally wet weather, and terrain difficulties. November 1944 saw twice as much rainfall as normal, limiting Allied air support, and considerably diminishing the mobility of US Army tank units. The focus of the 12th Army Group attacks in the First US Army sector consisted of two very different types of terrain: the congested, urbanized Aachen–Stolberg corridor, and the forested and hilly Hürtgen Forest that abutted the Ardennes. Bradley stubbornly continued the push in the Hürtgen Forest as the simplest means to reach the Roer dams. Allied planners had belatedly recognized that the dams posed a unique hazard to operations on the Roer plains approaching the Rhine, since the Germans could open the floodgates and flood the plains in the midst of Allied operations.

Bradley meets with Maj. Gen. Walter Robinson, commander of the 2nd Infantry Division, at the Eagle Tactical HQ on November 8, 1944. The defense of the Elsenborn Ridge by Robertson's division in December 1944 was a key ingredient in the defeat of the main 6. Panzerarmee thrust. (NARA)

By early November, Bradley became convinced that the Germans beyond the Aachen–Stolberg corridor were in a weakened state comparable to German forces in Normandy prior to Operation *Cobra*. He devised a plan called Operation *Queen* that would start with a carpet-bombing of German forward defenses, followed by a breakthrough and a mechanized exploitation towards the Roer. The Allied intelligence assessment was fundamentally mistaken. German forces in the Aachen–Stolberg corridor were indeed weak, but only because Hitler had ordered the

Battle of attrition, September 16–December 15, 1944

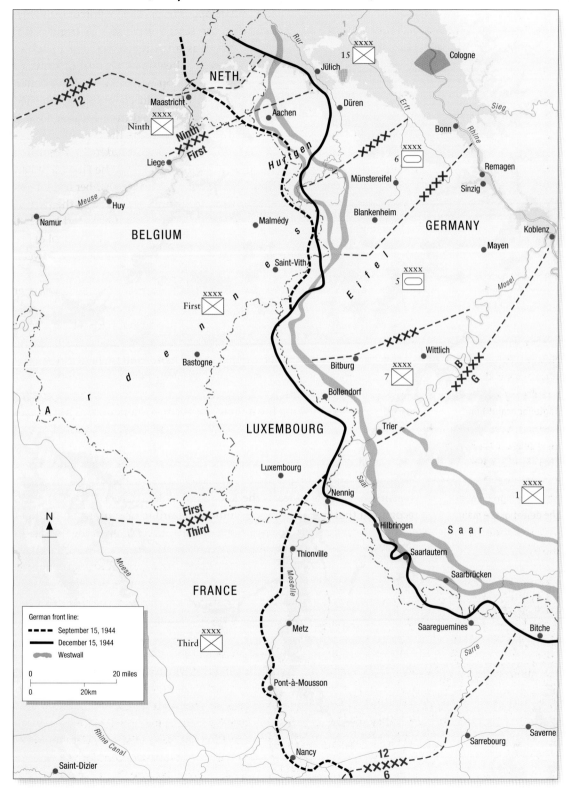

German front line:
- **– – –** September 15, 1944
- **———** December 15, 1944
- Westwall

0   20 miles
0   20km

NETH.

Cologne
Jülich
15
Düren
Aachen
Bonn
Remagen
Münstereifel
Sinzig
6
Blankenheim
Liege
Malmédy
Huy
GERMANY
Koblenz
Namur
BELGIUM
Mayen
Saint-Vith
5
First
Eifel
Bastogne
Wittlich
Bitburg
7
Bollendorf
LUXEMBOURG
Trier
Luxembourg
1
Nennig
Hilbringen
Saar
Saarlautern
Thionville
Saarbrücken
FRANCE
Third
Metz
Saareguemines
Bitche
Pont-à-Mousson
Sarrebourg
Saverne
Saint-Dizier
Nancy
12
6

Maastricht
Ninth
Ninth
First

21
12

Hurtgen

Ardennes

Meuse
Muese
Moselle
Saar
Rhine
Sieg
Erft
Rur
Mosel
Sarre
Rhine Canal

First
Third

B
G

N

41

Bradley visits the
4th Armored Division
Headquarters in
Château-Salins on
November 13 to talk with
the XII Corps commanders.
From left to right are
Maj. Gen. Willard Paul
(26th Division), Bradley,
Maj. Gen. John Woods
(4th Armored Division),
and Maj. Gen. Manton Eddy
(XII Corps). (NARA)

best forces pulled back into the Eifel to prepare for the surprise Ardennes offensive in December. Whenever the defenses in this area were seriously threatened by American advances, Hitler dipped into the Ardennes reserve and temporarily remedied the situation. Operation *Queen* began on November 16. After three weeks of intense fighting, three of the four corps taking part in the operation had reached most of their objectives along the Roer River. Unfortunately, it was the main push by Collins' VII Corps which had failed to meet its objective, due in no small measure to the intractability of the Hürtgen defenses. US forces finally fought their way out of the Hürtgen Forest, but at horrible cost, and the progress of Operation *Queen* fell far below Bradley's expectations. The First US Army exited the forest without enough strength to push on to Düren, and the offensive failed to solve the problem posed by the Roer dams.

The Siegfried Line campaign in the autumn of 1944 was one of the most costly fought by the US Army during World War II with about 48,000 battle casualties, including at least 8,250 killed in action. About half these casualties were incurred in the Hürtgen Forest. As an attritional campaign, it smashed up six German divisions and hampered German efforts to rebuild its forces prior to the Ardennes offensive. The Wehrmacht lost over 12,000 killed in the forest fighting, and many more prisoners and wounded. Bradley's operations in the Aachen corridor were more skillful and successful than the Hürtgen battles, but the territorial gains were not particularly impressive – the deepest penetration into Germany by the First and Ninth US Armies after crossing the German frontier was only 22 miles. Eisenhower's limited objective in the autumn of 1944 was to tie down the Wehrmacht in an attritional battle until logistics were ready for a renewed offensive in 1945; in this respect the campaign had positive results. During the autumn fighting, the Wehrmacht lost 95,000 men to the First and Ninth US Armies in prisoners alone, and other battle casualties were comparable to US losses.

In contrast to the limited gains enjoyed by Simpson's Ninth US Army and Hodge's First US Army, Patton's Third US Army conducted a brief and successful campaign in Lorraine. The Third US Army was constrained by Eisenhower's moratorium until mid-November, and then launched Operation *Madison* to clear the fortified Metz area. The focus of the attack was in Maj. Gen. Walton Walker's XX Corps sector, and in spite of the atrocious weather, the "Ghost Corps" methodically ground through the fortified belts and pushed on to the Westwall along the Saar River on the German frontier. Patton's forces had severely mauled the German AOK 1 and were planning an early winter offensive towards Mainz and Mannheim codenamed Operation *Tink* that was scheduled to begin on December 19.

The Ardennes debacle

Patton's Third US Army fought its autumn battles almost completely disconnected from the other two field armies of Bradley's 12th Army Group. The gap between them was the Ardennes. Bradley kept the Ardennes thinly covered by Middleton's VIII Corps, and, in December 1944, this consisted of two green divisions freshly arrived from the United States, and two other divisions which were being rebuilt after having been bled white in the Hürtgen fighting. Bradley felt that the weak coverage of the Ardennes front was a necessary risk given the unlikelihood of major German actions in this sector.

One of Bradley's primary dictums as a commander was to envision the battle from the enemy perspective. The problem with his execution of this rule was that it generally meant placing himself in the position of his German opponent and then seeing how the terrain and other factors would shape the forthcoming battlefield. While there was nothing especially wrong in such a prescription, the perceptions of the erstwhile Generalfeldmarschall Bradley were not necessarily the same as those of the actual German commanders. Bradley was a cautious planner and had a less instinctive grasp of the German perspective than someone like Patton, who was a risk-taker closer in temperament to many German commanders. Furthermore, the Ardennes attack had not been developed by the senior German field commanders, who in many cases shared Bradley's view that it was too risky. The Ardennes attack was the brainchild of Hitler himself, who saw it as a last desperate gamble.

Bradley's shortsightedness was amplified by shortcomings in Allied intelligence. The Ultra signals intelligence effort had provided senior Allied commanders with an almost steady stream of tactical and operational intelligence, and there was the inevitable tendency to ignore potential operations that had never been manifest in the Ultra traffic. Allied intelligence chiefs were well aware that Germany's contraction of defense lines in late 1944 led to greater use of teletype, telephones, and personal meetings that were not visible to their signals intelligence collection methods based on radio transmission, so there remained the problem of identifying "the dog that did not bark." The Ardennes was a classic case of this problem, since Hitler imposed a strict quarantine on information about the plans, and extensive steps were taken to camouflage the transfer and deployment of German units taking part in the attacks.

Nevertheless, there was ample tactical evidence. The Wehrmacht was hoarding forces behind the main line of resistance, and these units showed up on Allied assessments of German order of battle. The key issue was the interpretation of what these deployments meant. Rather than seeing them as a potential element in a

Bradley was unhappy with the poor discipline in the 1st Division, and its commander, Terry Allen, was relieved from the command on Sicily in 1943. Allen returned to the US, was assigned to train the new 104th Division, and returned to the ETO in the autumn of 1944. The division won the reputation of being one of the best of the new wave divisions owing to Allen's realistic training regime, and was particularly famous for its use of night-fighting tactics. (NARA)

surprise attack, Bradley, as well as key G-2 officers at SHAEF, 12th Army Group, and First US Army, all came to the consensus that the Wehrmacht was massing its forces to counterattack the Allies during their attack towards the Rhine sometime in early 1945. This was an entirely plausible interpretation in view of the conservative and risk-averse command style of senior Allied commanders such as Bradley and Montgomery. However, it simply wasn't true. Eisenhower's G-2, Gen. Kenneth Strong, began to have some concerns over the threat to the Ardennes in the weeks preceding the attack, but Bradley continued to downplay the risk due to the rough terrain conditions and sodden weather in the Ardennes in the early winter months. One of the few senior G-2 officers to voice concerns that something wasn't quite right was Patton's G-2, Oscar Koch. When Patton's Third US Army pushed over the Saar River in December 1944, it was greeted by the usual local counterattacks. But the German reinforcement effort in the Saar was not commensurate to the threat posed by Patton's Third US Army in late December 1944, especially with so many reinforcements readily available nearby in the Eifel. Not only had Patton's forces crossed the Saar, but Devers' 6th Army Group had reached the Rhine in Alsace without provoking much in the way of reinforcement. This suggested that the Germans were planning some sort of operation with these forces sooner rather than later. Both Patton and Koch promoted these views to senior commanders including Bradley, but to little avail.

Bradley was at Ike's SHAEF HQ in Versailles when the Germans attacked on December 16. At first, Bradley saw the first reports of the attacks as nothing more than a local diversion, but it soon became apparent that a major attack was underway when 16 German divisions were identified and when Generalfeldmarschall von Rundstedt's order of the day was translated. Bradley requested and received the two SHAEF reserve units, with the 101st Airborne being directed to Bastogne and the 82nd Airborne to the Malmedy area. Eisenhower ordered Patton to free up the 10th Armored Division regardless of its commitment to Operation *Tink*, and the 7th and 9th Armored Divisions were ordered to move towards Saint-Vith. Bradley's G-2 (intelligence), Brig. Gen. Edwin Sibert, was later sacked.

The fate of the Ardennes offensive was decided in the first few days of the campaign, largely due to the failure of the German *Schwerpunkt* (main focus) of 6. Panzerarmee to break through the American defenses in the northern sector near the Elsenborn Ridge. This was the most dangerous avenue for the Allies since it provided the most direct route to the Meuse River crossings and to Antwerp. This part of the battle was won by the actions of local commanders in which Bradley and the senior commanders played little immediate role. The first and only major German success occurred in the 5. Panzerarmee sector when the green 106th Division was overrun, and this opened up a route towards Bastogne and the Meuse. While the German Panzer advance beyond Bastogne proved to be very alarming, it was ultimately pointless because it pointed away from the main objective of Antwerp.

On December 19, Eisenhower called together a conference in Verdun to discuss the future conduct of the battle. The premonitions of Patton's intelligence chief had prompted the Third US Army to prepare the groundwork for a potential strike northward, and Ike was at first shocked by Patton's promise to have a corps moving on Bastogne within a few days. Patton made it obvious that the scheme was no pipe dream, and Eisenhower again realized his prudence in keeping the old and troublesome warhorse in command of Third US Army instead of sending him home in ignominy after Sicily. While Patton's star began to rise due to his reactions to the Ardennes attack, both Bradley's and Hodge's began to wane. Hodges appeared tired and confused, and the decision to withdraw the First US Army Headquarters from Spa to Chaudfontaine only seemed to add to the chaos. Bradley's headquarters in Luxembourg City was eventually cut off from the First US Army HQ, and the communication network gradually failed. The situation deteriorated to the point that Ike's deputy, "Beetle" Smith, became convinced of the need to turn over command of the US units on the northern shoulder of the Bulge to Montgomery's 21st Army Group headquarters since they had direct communication links to First US Army HQ. Both Ike and Smith realized there would be a price to pay for such a decision. Montgomery had been pressuring Eisenhower to be appointed as the ETO land commander, and this move would only seem to reinforce his position. Such a command shift would be publicly seen as a slap to Bradley, so the shift was kept secret until later in the month. Bradley was left with only a rump of the 12th Army Group's force, mainly Patton's Third US Army and the remnants of the First US Army's divisions in the Bastogne sector. To add insult to injury, Montgomery called Bradley to a meeting at Christmas at the 21st Army Group headquarters where Montgomery went into another of his tirades about the failures of the US Army since Normandy. Bradley passively accepted these outbursts, exploding in fury when he returned to his own Headquarters. The Christmas meeting removed whatever respect Bradley still had for Montgomery, and he began to complain vociferously to Eisenhower.

Montgomery's control of the northern shoulder of the Bulge initially had a calming effect at First US Army Headquarters, and many US commanders felt that he did an excellent job of reducing the crisis in the days after the initial attack. However, his penchant for "tidying up" the battlefield and meticulously preparing future actions soon served to exasperate local American commanders who were itching to begin a counterattack. Montgomery attempted to halt portions of the attack by Collin's VII Corps to the north of Bastogne, notably the advance by the 2nd Armored Division towards the Meuse, and Bradley managed to stay in touch with First US Army officers to make certain that Collins was left with a free hand. Montgomery's orders to Collins were

Bradley meets Patton in Bastogne on February 5, 1945 to discuss the forthcoming Third US Army campaign to reduce the Vianden bulge in Luxembourg. (NARA)

delayed and Collin's counterattack smashed the 5. Panzerarmee spearhead in the Celles pocket in the days after Christmas.

Montgomery's laggard pace in preparing a counterattack, and yet another obnoxious letter to Ike on December 29 about his usual hobby horses of unified ground command and a single thrust to Berlin, brought the command crisis to a head. Eisenhower penned a letter to Marshall and the Joint Chiefs of Staff that made it clear the situation had become unbearable and that they would have to choose between him or Montgomery. In reality, Ike knew that he would be favored in any such decision, not only because of Marshall's support, but also because of Montgomery's alienation of many senior British commanders as well. In the event, Beetle gave Montgomery's aide a day to convince his boss of the gravity of the situation, and Montgomery responded with an uncharacteristically apologetic letter that temporarily defused the situation.

Besides leading to an even deeper chasm between Montgomery and the senior American commanders, the Ardennes altered Bradley's perceptions of Patton. With little more than the Third US Army under his command, Bradley was heartened by Patton's cooperativeness. Patton became Bradley's champion with the press. On January 17, when Hodge's First US Army met up with Patton's Third US Army at Houfallize, Bradley's 12th Army Group took back control of First US Army. The Ardennes fighting also convinced Bradley of the need to pay more attention to the press. He had been very naive about press affairs and there was no press contingent assigned to the 12th Army Group Headquarters in 1944. After seeing how effectively Montgomery and Patton manipulated the press to push their agendas, Bradley finally created a press office in his headquarters.

On to the Rhine

In the aftermath of the Ardennes fighting, the Allied armies began to prepare for the final assault towards the Rhine. Eisenhower had agreed to attach Simpson's Ninth US Army to Montgomery for the Rhine crossing operation, much to the consternation of Bradley who was left only with First and Third US Armies. As a way to mollify Brooke and the senior British leadership, Eisenhower had continued to accept their premise that the main thrust would come in Montgomery's northern sector, aimed at the northern portion of the Ruhr. Bradley continued to push for a broader range of options, and Eisenhower left open the door for major thrusts beyond Montgomery's Rhine crossing, which was dubbed Operation *Plunder*. February saw a return of late winter weather with omnipresent rain that left the Roer plain muddy and treacherous. First US Army began its effort to push past the Roer, while Patton's Third US Army slogged its way past the Vianden bulge in Luxembourg, clearing up the last of the German forces in this sector. Eisenhower's initial plan saw little potential for a Rhine crossing in the sector of the First US Army east of the Ardennes, and instead concentrated on possibilities in Patton's sector near Mainz–Mannheim with an eventual objective of Frankfurt. The main focus of the first phase of the

Rhine operation was to destroy as much of the Wehrmacht as possible on the west bank of the Rhine, exploiting Hitler's tendency to issue "no retreat" orders.

The first phase of the Anglo-American offensive began on February 8 with two operations aimed at closing on the Rhine in the northern sector. Operation *Veritable* was Montgomery's effort to push the 21st Army Group through the Reichswald and into position on the west bank of the Rhine for a major river-crossing operation. Operation *Grenade* was a supporting effort by the Ninth US Army to finally clear the Roer River and as a prelude to future operations along the Rhine. Bradley was not content to let First US Army sit idle through the month, and by late February he convinced Eisenhower to permit First US Army to assist Operation *Grenade* with a simultaneous crossing of the Roer on February 23 to protect the advance's southern flank.

Bradley and his field army commanders in March 1945 with George Patton (Third US Army) above him to the right, William Simpson (Ninth US Army) to the upper right, and Courtney Hodges (First US Army) to the lower right. (MHI)

Operation *Veritable* proved more difficult than anticipated due to the flooded terrain and stubborn German resistance. Operation *Grenade* made far better progress and on March 2, Simpson's Ninth US Army reached the Rhine at Neuss. Simpson pointed out to Eisenhower that nine of his 12 divisions were free to conduct a surprise crossing of the Rhine. Eisenhower again deferred to Montgomery, waiting for a crossing in the British sector.

With the first phase of the Allied offensive complete, Bradley received Eisenhower's permission for the First US Army to close on the Rhine. Operation *Lumberjack* began on March 1, 1945, with the aim of clearing the west bank of the Rhine from the Cologne area south, linking up with Patton's Third US Army on the Ahr River near Koblenz. Bradley put more emphasis on Patton's potential for a Rhine crossing, and Eisenhower supported this with Operation *Undertone*, an attack by Devers' 6th Army Group north through the Wissembourg Gap from Alsace along the Rhine, greatly weakening the German opposition in the Saar-Palatinate that faced Patton.

The March fighting made it clear that the Wehrmacht had suffered lethal blows in the Ardennes fighting. The Allied campaign to reach the Rhine in February and March 1945 cost the Wehrmacht about 400,000 casualties, including 280,000 prisoners. Besides these tangible losses, there was a palpable collapse in German morale and discipline as more and more officers and soldiers reached the conclusion that defeat was imminent. The spearhead for First US Army, Collins' VII Corps, began its attack across the Erft River on March 1, 1945, and proceeded on schedule against ineffective resistance. A cavalry reconnaissance patrol reached the Rhine north of Cologne on March 3, and the main assault into Cologne began on March 5 led by the tanks of the 3rd Armored Division and followed closely by the infantry of the 104th Division. Milliken's III Corps exited the gloom

Allied plans following the Battle of the Bulge, February 1945

NORTH SEA

Amsterdam

IJsselmeer

Zwolle

Ems

Osnabrück

NETHERLANDS

North German Plain

Münster

The Hague

Utrecht

Zutphen

Lek

Arnhem

IJssel

February 7, 1945

First Can.

Rotterdam

Dordrecht

Waal

Grave

Veritable

Plunder

Wesel

Lippe

Hamm

Breda

Tilburg

Second Br.

Ruhr

Essen

Dortmund

Duisburg

Hagen

Ruhr

GERMANY

XXXXX 21

Montgomery

Roermond

Maas

Niers

Düsseldorf

Antwerp

Albert Canal

Escaut-Meuse Canal

Demer

Roer

Grenade

Rhine

Ghent

January 15–28, 1945

Ninth

Erft

Cologne

Siegen

Giessen

Brussels

Dendre

Senne

Dyle

Maastricht

Aachen

Lumberjack

Düren

Euskirchen

Bonn

Sieg

Lahn

BELGIUM

Liege

First

Lumberjack

Remagen

Mons

Namur

Meuse

Koblenz

Sambre

December 26, 1944

Saint-Vith

Ardennes Offensive, December 16, 1944

Mayen

Wiesbaden

Frankfurt

December 16, 1944 to January 30, 1945

Dinant

Prüm

The Eifel

Mainz

Oppenheim

XXXXX 12

Bradley

Bastogne

Semois

LUX.

Our

Lumberjack

Moselle

Bad Kreuznach

Undertone

Mézières

Third

Trier

Worms

Sedan

Arlon

Mannheim

Rethel

Aisne

Luxembourg

Palatinate

Saar

Undertone

Kaiserslautern

Operation Nordwind, January 1, 1945

Reims

Verdun

Metz

Seventh

Saarbrücken

Châlons

Sarreguemines

Bitche

Wissembourg

Karlsruhe

Stuttgart

FRANCE

Lorraine

January 1–30, 1945

Haguenau

Baden-Baden

Saint-Dizier

Nancy

Sarrebourg

Strasbourg

First Fr.

Kehl

Marne

Toul

XXXXX 6

Lunéville

Sarre

Black Forest

Troyes

Devers

Neufchâteau

Saint-Die

Meurthe

Moselle

Colmar

Rhine

Freiburg

V o s g e s

January 20–February 9, 1945

Mulhouse

Belfort

Basel

Zurich

SWITZERLAND

Dijon

Besançon

| | Westwall |
| February 7, 1945 | Date of capture by Allied forces |

0 ——— 50 miles

0 ——— 50km

N

and the mud of the Eifel Forest and came out into the Cologne plains. The Germans expected Milliken to head for Bonn, but instead the corps began barreling down the undefended Rheinback Valley heading toward Remagen.

Luck strikes when opportunity meets preparation, and First US Army showed itself ready on March 7 when an artillery spotter plane noticed that the Germans had not demolished the railroad bridge at Remagen. A task force from 9th Armored Division raced to the bridge and began moving across when the Germans set off the demolition charges. The charges weakened the bridge but failed to drop it into the Rhine. The US Army had unexpectedly captured a major bridge over the Rhine weeks before Montgomery's planned Rhine crossing. The Remagen windfall prompted Bradley to dust off a plan he had conceived the previous autumn to exploit Patton's progress in Lorraine. Dubbed Operation *Voyage*, the scheme would encircle the Ruhr industrial zone with a northern pincer of Simpson's Ninth US Army, supported by a major advance by both First and Third US Armies along the southern side.

The capture of the bridge at Remagen fundamentally altered the planning for the final endgame against the Third Reich. Here at III Corps Headquarters, First US Army commander Courtney Hodges shows Ike, Bradley, and III Corps commander James Van Fleet the plans for the exploitation of the Remagen bridgehead. (MHI)

While Eisenhower would not immediately commit to Operation *Voyage*, Bradley's proposal convinced him to back away from an unlimited commitment to Montgomery's offensive. When Montgomery again pressed him with the extravagant demand for another ten US divisions for the already bloated Operation *Plunder*, Eisenhower cleverly conceded the point but on the condition that Bradley's 12th Army Group be given back control of all the Ninth and First US Army units scheduled to participate in *Plunder*. With his bluff called Montgomery backed off, preferring to have only the Ninth US Army under his control than to have double the US reinforcements but all under Bradley's command.

Eisenhower began to ponder Bradley's Operation *Voyage* scheme much more seriously because of the success of Operation *Undertone* in the middle of March. The Seventh US Army campaign broke through the Westwall fortifications in the Wissembourg Gap and began moving north up the west bank of the Rhine. Patton was itching to move on the Rhine, and pointed out that the Westwall defenses in the Saar could be outflanked if his Third US Army bounced the Moselle and Saar rivers and raced for the Rhine, effectively cutting off the German Heeresgruppe G from the rear. Hitler's refusal to countenance any withdrawals from west of the Rhine left the Heeresgruppe G defenses vulnerable. Although many senior US commanders dismissed the promised offensive as Patton's usual bravado, Bradley saw the merit of the plan and pushed for it hard with Eisenhower.

In the pre-dawn hours of March 13, two of Patton's corps began their preliminary bombardment; the ensuing lightning advance into the Saar-Palatinate in the two middle weeks of March was dubbed the "Rhine Rat Race" by the GIs of the Third US Army after the German units in the area collapsed and began racing back to the Rhine. The German main line of resistance from Trier to Koblenz was pushed all the way back to a line from Mannheim to Mainz on the Rhine, and most of the German AOK 7 was destroyed in the process. It recalled the heady days of August 1944 when Patton's Third US Army had raced to Paris. Third Army estimated that the opposing German forces had lost 113,000 men in two weeks of fighting, including 68,000 prisoners, compared to US casualties of only 5,220. Seventh US Army and attached French units captured 22,000 Germans and estimated that the opposing German formations had lost 75–80 percent of their infantry. As importantly, the advance had placed Third US Army along the Rhine, and Patton had already hoarded plenty of tactical bridging for precisely such an opportunity.

The spectacular success of Operation *Undertone* reinforced Eisenhower's preference for a broad-front strategy in the endgame against Germany, and undermined his commitment to Montgomery's Operation *Plunder* as the primary Allied thrust. The collapse of the Wehrmacht in the Saar-Palatinate was evidence that the Wehrmacht was in crisis and could not hold such an extended front. While Montgomery slowly prepared Operation *Plunder*, the southern group of US field armies had shattered Heeresgruppe G and gained access to central and southern Germany. Eisenhower would let *Plunder* proceed, but on March 19, he gave Bradley the green light for Operation *Voyage*. Eisenhower's strategic changes in Allied war planning in the last two weeks of March were prompted by several related factors. The elephantine extravaganza of Operation *Plunder* was a reminder of Montgomery's cautious and laborious tactical style. While this approach might have been prudent when the Wehrmacht was at its prime, it was excessively timid when the Wehrmacht was disintegrating. The contrast with Bradley's 12th Army Group was striking; Patton's aggressive Saar-Palatinate campaign helped to shatter Heeresgruppe G, and Bradley was promising much the same fate for Heeresgruppe B with Operation *Voyage*. Eisenhower recognized that the US Army commanders had adapted to the opportunities presented by the crisis in the Wehrmacht. They were advocating and carrying out bold operations that exploited the brittle German defenses while Montgomery was slow to adapt. Instead of the British 21st Army Group conducting the Ruhr encirclement, the task went instead to Bradley's 12th Army Group.

Ike, Bradley, Hodges, and Collins meet at the Kurhotel in Petersberg overlooking the Rhine on March 26, 1945 to discuss the breakout from the Remagen bridgehead. (NARA)

As a preliminary step to Operation *Voyage*, Bradley authorized Patton's Third US Army to cross the Rhine, setting the stage for a broader right hook to the northwest. Late on the evening of March 22, a regiment of the 5th Infantry Division crossed near Nierstein and three more regiments quickly followed. A 40-ton treadway bridge was erected by the afternoon of March 23. To needle Montgomery, Bradley announced the success of the crossing the day before Montgomery's planned operation, pointing out that the 12th Army Group could cross the Rhine even without artillery preparation, never mind an airborne assault.

Operation *Voyage* began a day after Operation *Plunder* on March 25, 1945. Both First and Third US Armies led with strong armored forces and the weather permitted extensive air support. Within a day, the German defenses were disintegrating. The northern arm of the Ruhr encirclement was the Ninth US Army, still subordinate to Montgomery's Operation *Plunder*. The US Army portion of the attack, dubbed Operation *Flashpoint*, was initiated in the pre-dawn hours of March 25. The Rhine crossings around Wesel proceeded with little difficulty.

By March 28, the progress opposite the Remagen bridgehead had been so impressive that Bradley began refining the movements of Operation *Voyage*. Hodges' First US Army was directed to swing northward, with the objective being Paderborn, while Patton's Third US Army was directed to the northeast, aiming at Kassel. The First US Army spearhead became entangled with German Panzer forces around Paderborn, but on March 31, Collins' VII Corps began coordinating with the Ninth US Army to conduct a link-up. Shortly after midnight on Easter Sunday, April 1, CCB of 2nd Armored Division from Ninth US Army sent one of its task forces towards Lippstadt while shortly before dawn, Task Force Kane from 3rd Armored Division, First US Army, set out for Lippstadt from the opposite direction. By 1530hrs, the two US task forces made first contact near Lippstadt encircling the Ruhr pocket.

The operational objective of Operation *Voyage* was to encircle the Ruhr in order to cut off its military industries. Bradley assumed that about 70,000 troops would be left in the pocket but that most of Heeresgruppe B had already made their escape. Bradley had not counted on Hitler's stand-fast orders and in fact, the pocket contained about 370,000 German troops, most of the remains of Heeresgruppe B. Although German commanders had urged Hitler to withdraw the main elements of Heeresgruppe B from the Ruhr in order to continue the fight from more tenable positions in central Germany, on March 28 Hitler had announced that the Ruhr industrial region was now designated as "Festung Ruhr," and therefore there would

Eisenhower had been pushing for Bradley's fourth star since December 1944, and here his two aides, Maj. Lewis Bridge (left) and Maj. Chet Hansen (right) are seen pinning them on in a ceremony at Namur, Belgium, on April 1, 1945. Hansen was a long-serving aide to Bradley after the war as well, and was the ghost-writer behind Bradley's 1951 autobiography. (MHI)

be no retreat; Heeresgruppe B would fight or die. Hitler expected that Army Group B could last for months using the industrial resources in the Ruhr.

On the evening of March 28, control of the Ninth US Army reverted from Montgomery's 21st Army Group to Bradley's 12th Army Group to provide a unified command for the reduction of the Ruhr pocket. Furthermore, a new field army, the Fifteenth US Army, was already underway to the Ruhr where it would be used to bottle up the pocket and conduct occupation duties. Following the Ruhr encirclement, Bradley's primary focus was eastward towards the Elbe River to link up with the Red Army.

By mid-April, with the situation hopeless, Heeresgruppe B disbanded itself rather than formally surrender; its commander, Generalfeldmarschall Walther Model, committed suicide. The pocket largely collapsed by April 18. In total, some 317,000 German troops surrendered in the Ruhr, a greater total than even Stalingrad or Tunisia. The destruction of Heeresgruppe B in the Ruhr pocket marked the end of large-scale operations by the Wehrmacht in the west, leading to what the new commander Albert Kesselring called the "makeshift campaign" – a disjointed effort of local defensive actions conducted by what few divisions had sufficient morale to continue the fight under such hopeless circumstances. The war would go on for another few weeks, but the outcome by now was obvious.

Beyond the Ruhr encirclement, the Allies were obliged to decide how to conduct the final endgame against Germany. Montgomery and the British Chiefs of Staff continued to push for a northern focus in the final campaign in Germany, and still held hopes for an assault towards Berlin. This was unlikely for several reasons, both tactical and strategic. Roosevelt, Churchill, and Stalin had already agreed that Berlin would be within the Soviet zone of occupation; at the beginning of April the Red Army was only 40 miles from Berlin at the time compared to the 200–300 miles of the 21st Army Group. Given his conservative command style, the idea that Montgomery could execute a lightning strike towards Berlin was more than a little preposterous. Since the mission might be foisted on Bradley's 12th Army Group, Eisenhower turned to him for advice. Bradley estimated it would cost 100,000 casualties which Eisenhower judged "a pretty stiff price for a prestige objective." Actual Soviet casualties in the Berlin operation were 352,000 including 78,000 killed. In late March, Eisenhower made it clear that the Berlin option had been rejected.

The ultimate dividing line with the approaching Red Army in April was the Elbe River in the north and the Mulde River in the south. Simpson's Ninth US Army first reached the river on April 12 near Tangermunde, 53 miles from Berlin. On April 15, Simpson conferred with Bradley about making a thrust for Berlin, but Eisenhower instructed them to consolidate their positions and wait for the Red Army. Bradley's focus in the last half of April was the south, especially Bavaria. Allied intelligence was worried that the Germans would fall back into an Alpine redoubt to make their last stand in the Bavarian Alps south of Munich, where the Nazi movement was first born. As a result, Patton's Third US Army was directed southeastward in the

Encircling the Ruhr, March 29–April 4, 1945

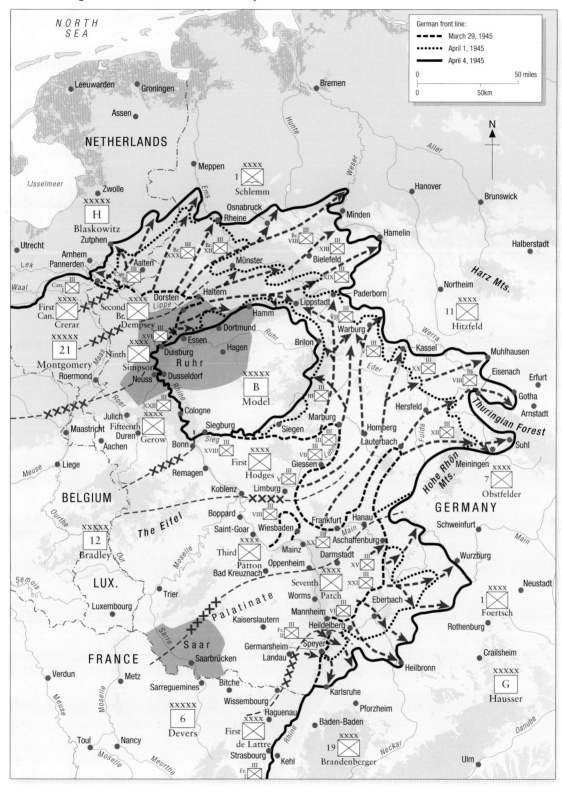

German front line:
- – – – March 29, 1945
- ·········· April 1, 1945
- ——— April 4, 1945

0   50 miles
0   50km

N

NORTH SEA

NETHERLANDS

Leeuwarden   Groningen
Assen
Meppen
Bremen
Hanover
Brunswick
IJsselmeer
Zwolle
1 Schlemm
Osnabruck
Minden
Hamelin
Halberstadt

H
Blaskowitz
Zutphen
Rheine
Bielefeld
Utrecht
Arnhem
Pannerden
Aalten
Münster
Paderborn
Northeim
11 Hitzfeld
Harz Mts.

Waal
Lek
First Can. Crerar
Second Br. Dempsey
Dorsten
Haltern
Lippe
Lippstadt
Hamm
Warburg
Kassel
Muhlhausen
Eisenach
Erfurt

21 Montgomery
Maas
Roermond
Ninth Simpson
Neuss
Essen
Dortmund
Duisburg
Ruhr
Hagen
Brilon
Ruhr
Eder
Werra

B Model

Dusseldorf
Cologne
Siegburg
Siegen
Marburg
Homberg
Lauterbach
Hersfeld
Gotha
Arnstadt
Thuringian Forest
Suhl

Julich
Maastricht
Duren
Aachen
Fifteenth Gerow
Bonn
Remagen
Sieg
Giessen
Lahn
Meuse
Liege
First Hodges
Limburg
Koblenz
Meiningen
7 Obstfelder
Hohe Rhön Mts.

BELGIUM
Ourthe
The Eifel
Boppard
Saint-Goar
Wiesbaden
Frankfurt
Hanau
Schweinfurt
GERMANY
Main

12 Bradley
Our
Moselle
Mainz
Darmstadt
Aschaffenburg
Wurzburg
Neustadt

LUX.
Luxembourg
Trier
Third Patton
Oppenheim
Bad Kreuznach
Semois
Seventh Patch
Worms
Mannheim
Eberbach
1 Foertsch
Rothenburg

Verdun
Metz
Sarreguemines
Bitche
Kaiserslautern
Palatinate
Heildelberg
Speyer
Heilbronn
Crailsheim

FRANCE
Saar
Saarbrücken
Germarsheim
Landau
Karlsruhe
Pforzheim
G Hausser

6 Devers
Wissembourg
Haguenau
First de Lattre
Strasbourg
Baden-Baden
19 Brandenberger
Danube

Toul
Nancy
Moselle
Meurthe
Kehl
Rhine
Neckar
Ulm

Verdun
Meuse

last two weeks of April 1945 to clear out any potential resistance centers. In fact there was no scheme for a national redoubt, but the effort pushed Patton's forces into northwest Austria near Obersalzburg and Linz, and across the Czechoslovak border. Bradley ordered Patton to hold his forces on the Moldau River. With nearly all of Germany overrun and Hitler dead, the remnants of the German government sued for peace by the end of the first week of May 1945.

Following the German surrender, Bradley's 12th Army Group was disbanded. Hodges' First US Army and Simpson's Ninth US Army were slated for the Pacific Theater and the final assault on Japan, Patton's Third US Army was to remain on occupation duty in Europe. Bradley expected to be recalled to Washington.

Bradley toasts Marshal Ivan Konev, commander of the 1st Ukrainian Front, at his headquarters near Torgau on May 5, 1945 after US and Soviet forces had met along the Elbe River. (MHI)

OPPOSING COMMANDERS

The enormous scale of World War II seldom provided the neat symmetries of "Napoleon versus Wellington at Waterloo." Allied coalition warfare constrained Bradley's freedom of action within the broader ambitions of Allied operational plans. Likewise, Bradley's German opponents were usually limited by Hitler's schemes. Their merits as commanders can only be judged by their achievements within these confines and their success or failure at utilizing the qualities of their armies to the fullest.

Bradley's opponents while in command of II Corps in Tunisia were parts of General der Panzertruppen Gustav von Vaerst's 5. Panzerarmee. This army was under strength and not organized in a conventional fashion, so there was no corresponding corps commander facing Bradley's II Corps. Certainly the most prominent commander in this sector, though not well known at the time, was Generalmajor Erich von Manteuffel, commander of the improvised "Division Manteuffel." However, Manteuffel was evacuated for medical reasons at the end of March and replaced by Generalleutnant Karl Bülowius.

Much the same was the case during the Sicily campaign. During the opening amphibious assault phase of Operation *Husky*, Bradley's II Corps was nominally opposed by the XVI Corpo d'Armata commanded by Generale di corpo Carlo Rossi. In reality, German units such as Panzer-Division "Hermann Göring" operated autonomously in the initial counterattacks. Following the beachhead battles around Gela, and Patton's subsequent drive into western Sicily, Bradley's II Corps faced a variety of German and Italian units under German command, but these forces never had a formal corps structure or single sector commander.

During Operation *Overlord* in June 1944, Bradley's First US Army was opposed by LXXXIV Infanterie Korps commanded by General der Infanterie

Erich Marcks. He was widely regarded as one of the best Wehrmacht general staff officers but was not favored by Berlin for political reasons. Ironically, during the anti-invasion staff exercises for senior Normandy commanders in Rennes scheduled for June 6, Marcks had been assigned the role of the senior Allied commander. Marcks did not agree with Rommel about the tactics to defeat an Allied amphibious landing, since he felt that his forces were far too weak and thinly spread to defend the extensive coastline that his corps had been assigned. Although he led German forces during the first week of Normandy fighting, he was killed during an air attack on June 12. His place was taken by General der Infanterie Dietrich von Choltitz. He had begun the war as an infantry battalion commander in the Polish campaign, receiving the Iron Cross; he was decorated again with the Knight's Cross for his performance in the 1940 campaign in France. After his regiment's performance in the siege of Sevastopol in the summer of 1942, he rose to divisional command in August

1942, followed by corps command in December 1942. In early 1944, he was transferred to Italy to lead LXXVI Panzerkorps during the attempts to crush the Anzio beachhead. Choltitz was an extremely capable officer and, in spite of the modest forces available at his disposal, he managed to exploit the defensive features of the Normandy countryside to their fullest. After Operation *Cobra* finally overwhelmed his corps, Choltitz was given the hopeless task of commanding the Paris garrison where he surrendered later in August 1944.

By mid-September 1944, Bradley's enlarged 12th Army Group had pushed all the way to the German frontier near Aachen, and well into Lorraine around Nancy. Generalfeldmarschall Walther Model's Heeresgruppe B covered the sector from Dusseldorf to Trier, closely corresponding to Bradley's 12th Army Group. Model was one of Germany's most skilled field commanders, and a master of defensive warfare. Model had become Hitler's miracle worker and when all seemed hopeless and defeat inevitable, Hitler called on this energetic and ruthless commander to save the day. After a distinguished career as a Panzer commander during the Russian campaign, in March 1944 he became the Wehrmacht's youngest field marshal. When Heeresgruppe Mitte was shattered by the Red Army's Operation *Bagration* in the summer of 1944, Model was appointed by Hitler to the nearly hopeless task of restoring order, which he accomplished in the midst of chaos with very modest reinforcements. In mid-August, after German forces in France had been surrounded in the Falaise Gap, Hitler recalled Model from the Eastern Front and assigned him command of Heeresgruppe B. The rout of the German Army from France was so enormous that senior Wehrmacht commanders dubbed the period from mid-August to mid-September 1944 "the Void." Model pulled off another miracle and retrieved a hopeless situation yet again. Surplus Luftwaffe and Kriegsmarine personnel were hastily reorganized into infantry units and positioned along the abandoned

Bradley's immediate counterpart during most of the fighting in the ETO was Generalfeldmarschall Walther Model, commander of Heeresgruppe B. Model was Germany's master of defense in 1944–45, overseeing the stabilization of the Russian Front in the early summer of 1944 after the Red Army's decisive victory during Operation *Bagration*. He was transferred to the west in August 1944 to help the Wehrmacht recover from its crippling defeats in Normandy. Model is seen here with SS-Oberstgruppenführer Josef "Sepp" Dietrich who commanded 6. Panzerarmee, the spearhead of the Ardennes offensive in December 1944. (MHI)

Westwall where they were instructed to "defend or die." By the end of September, the Allies' irreversible march to Berlin had come to an abrupt end, in no small measure due to Model's defensive talents.

The autumn campaign was another test of Model's abilities to extract every ounce of defensive value from his beleaguered forces. Hitler was insistent on building up a counterattack force for his secret Ardennes offensive, and so Berlin was miserly in allotting reinforcements to Heeresgruppe B. Model could not prevent the fall of Aachen, but he did succeed in extracting a high cost for the attritional battles along the Westwall in October–November 1944, especially in the grim battles in the Hürtgen Forest. Model was aided in his defensive mission by the soggy autumn weather that limited the value of Allied advantages in air power and tank mobility; the Allied supply problems also contributed to the stalemate.

As was the case with the other senior German commanders, Model had no input into the Ardennes plan and considered it "damned fragile." But he tried to execute the plan to the best of his ability. The attrition along the Westwall in the autumn of 1944 had badly weakened Heeresgruppe B, and the Allied bombing campaign had severely limited the Wehrmacht's ability to build up a sufficient reserve to overwhelm Bradley's 12th Army Group. After the failures of the first week of the Ardennes offensive prior to Christmas 1944, the plan was doomed. Regardless of the failure, Model continued to doggedly attempt to reinvigorate the offensive by carefully shifting his limited resources, but Bradley was able to exploit American advantages in mobility and air power to crush these efforts. The Ardennes fighting so weakened Heeresgruppe B that the best that Model could accomplish was to delay the inevitable advance of the US Army into Germany. Under relentless pressure from Bradley's forces in the Rhineland in March 1945, Model was careless in ensuring the protection of the final Rhine bridgeheads. The capture of the Ludendorff Bridge at Remagen led to the encirclement of Heeresgruppe B in the Ruhr pocket, and Model's death by his own hand. Like many German commanders of his generation, Model had a narrow perspective on his duties to Germany, equating German interests to Hitler's ambitions. In the end, Model's unquestioning loyalty to the Hitler regime and his success at delaying the inevitable Allied victory simply ensured that Germany was subjected to several more weeks or months of war, and the gruesome butcher's bill that the delay entailed.

WHEN WAR IS DONE

Following the end of the war in Europe, President Harry Truman decided that he needed an "outstanding Army figure" to clean up the problems in the Veterans Administration (VA). Since Eisenhower was being groomed to take over the Army chief-of-staff position, Bradley was the most likely candidate. Truman had his eye on Bradley in any event, as the popular journalist Ernie

Pyle had continued to laud him as "the GI General," and Truman wanted a commander more sympathetic to average GIs than someone like Patton. The VA post, while outside the usual career track for a senior American commander, had taken on exceptional importance since it was a key element in plans to reintegrate the large draftee army back into civilian life through the new "GI Bill." Eisenhower assured Bradley that he would press for his assignment as Army chief-of-staff at a later date, and Bradley agreed to the VA post. The VA required Bradley to become enmeshed in national politics, as the post held control over numerous sources of political patronage and controlled an exceptionally large budget. Bradley

was called upon to oversee a vast new program of insurance, education loans, home loans, and medical treatment. Truman and Bradley worked well together, even if they did not share the same viewpoints on defense issues. Both were from Missouri farm families, and both had political viewpoints heavily shaped by the prairie populist movements of the early 20th century.

Bradley took on his new tasks with the usual professionalism, but he remained first and foremost a military leader not a civil administrator. Truman wanted him to stay in the post at least two years to assure stability, but at the same time Eisenhower was anxious to leave the Army chief-of-staff post in hopes of retirement. In November 1947, Bradley was nominated as the Army chief-of-staff, and Congress approved this in early 1948. The Army was in a state of considerable turmoil in the post-war period. The US Army Air Force had finally been broken off as a separate service in 1947, and the former War Department was in the throes of extensive reorganization under the new Secretary of Defense, James Forrestal. The Cold War had started, and US Army forces in Europe were shifting from occupation duty to a new role in the defense of Europe against their erstwhile ally, the Soviet Union. The Army had been substantially downsized since the war, and was barely capable of conducting its occupation duties. Bradley later complained that in 1948 "it could not fight its way out of a paper bag." Bradley pushed for several new initiatives to meet the challenges facing the Army, including a program of universal military training and federalization of the National Guard. The largest debate centered over future defense spending, which had been sharply curtailed under the Truman administration. The budget remained far below the levels that Bradley considered prudent, and he later admitted that one of his greatest mistakes in the post-war years was not fighting more forcefully for needed increases. The culmination in the reorganization of the Department of Defense was the creation of a chairman of the Joint Chiefs of Staff, an attempt to impose a joint command over the squabbling branches of the armed forces. Truman appointed Bradley as the first chairman of the JCS in August 1949.

Bradley is sworn in as Eisenhower's replacement as Army chief-of-staff on February 1948. Behind them are President Harry Truman and Secretary of the Army Kenneth Royall. (MHI)

Bradley as Army chief-of-staff in 1948. (MHI)

The shortcomings in the US armed forces became painfully evident when North Korea invaded South Korea in June 1950. The Army in the Pacific was in particularly poor shape, and emergency measures were needed to build up an adequate counterattack force, even against as puny an adversary as North Korea. Besides his role as chairman of the JCS, Bradley was also appointed as the first chairman of the NATO Military Committee in 1950, part of a worldwide effort aimed at the containment of Soviet military power.

Overall command of the Korean effort was under Gen. Douglas MacArthur, the Pacific Theater commander based in Tokyo. Unlike Eisenhower, Bradley had had very little professional contact with MacArthur over the years. Command of army forces in Korea was originally entrusted to Gen. Walton "Bulldog" Walker, commander of XX Corps under Patton during the war. Walker was an aggressive and domineering commander who helped reorganize the army in Korea after the initial setbacks, but he had a quick falling out with MacArthur over tactics.

Although MacArthur had been instrumental in rallying the defense of Korea, he was at the same time extremely independent and began taking actions without consulting either Bradley or Truman, trampling the usual civilian–military boundaries. Truman began to consider replacing MacArthur with Bradley in August 1950 over MacArthur's actions in defense of Formosa (Taiwan) that had not been approved by the US government. Truman maneuvered to pull Marshall out of retirement to add more heft to the Washington defense establishment, and he became Secretary of Defense in September 1950 after a bruising confirmation process. Bradley was given his fifth star the same month at Truman's urging, equal in rank to MacArthur. Bradley showed little enthusiasm for MacArthur's Inchon landing scheme in Korea, but when it succeeded in September 1950 it only served to reinforce MacArthur's inclination towards actions independent of Washington.

Bradley later described the months of November–December 1950 as "the most trying of my military career, more so than the Bulge. The war in Korea abruptly turned from victory to humiliating defeat." Bradley, MacArthur, and most of the Washington establishment had seriously misjudged Chinese intentions. By November, the Chinese People's Volunteer Army (CPV) had begun to intervene in Korea after the US Army had pushed north of the 38th Parallel. In December 1950, small-scale actions had turned to a full-scale Chinese invasion that quickly overran the lead elements of the US Eighth Army in North Korea. US forces were routed and in a headlong retreat back south of the 38th Parallel. The abrupt reversal of fortune in Korea raised the specter of all-out war with China, a prospect that Truman and Bradley wished to avoid. American policy hoped to restore the balance in Korea after the Chinese intervention, but at the same time, to try to avoid an escalation of the fighting outside the Korean Peninsula.

Growing disagreements emerged between Washington and MacArthur, even after the front stabilized in January 1951. Walker's death in a traffic accident led to Matthew Ridgway taking his place as the army commander in Korea under MacArthur. Ridgway was an old friend of Bradley from his days with the 82nd Division, and Ridgway was instrumental in restoring the army's defensive lines in Korea in early 1951. By the early spring, the United Nations forces in Korea were going back over to the offensive. The final breakdown in relations with MacArthur came in late March 1951 after he released a communiqué suggesting that Beijing might want to negotiate with him over the future of the conflict. He had already been warned by Truman not to issue policy statements, and instead he had deliberately attempted to undercut Truman's forthcoming communication with Beijing with his own missive that conflicted with established US policy. By March 24, Truman had decided he could no longer tolerate MacArthur's insubordination, and he raised the issue with senior leaders including Bradley on April 6. Neither Bradley nor Marshall thought that MacArthur's actions were a clear-cut case of insubordination, and neither relished the idea of MacArthur's relief for fear that it would lead to politicization of the military command. On April 9, Truman made it clear that he favored MacArthur's relief and asked Bradley for his suggestions as a replacement; Bradley suggested Ridgway, who had performed admirably in command of Army units in Korea since December 1950. The decision was affirmed and Truman made a public announcement about the controversy on April 11, 1951. MacArthur was still enormously popular in the United States, and his ousting led to a series of bitter Congressional investigations by Truman's opponents. Bradley continued to stress the need to keep an eye on the broader strategic picture, and insisted that a full-scale war with China would be the "wrong war, at the wrong place, and the wrong time, and with the wrong enemy."

While the US government was attempting to reach a diplomatic solution to the Korean conflict, the Cold War continued to intensify in Europe. Bradley had hoped to retire after a single four-year term as JCS chairman, but under the circumstances he accepted Truman's request to remain for a second term starting in August 1951. The stalemate in Korea had led to the rebirth of the isolationist wing of the Republican Party, and in view of Truman's growing unpopularity a Republican victory in 1952 seemed likely. The leading candidate of the isolationist wing was Robert Taft, and his potential accession to the White House deeply worried Eisenhower and many others. Although apolitical until this point, Eisenhower was easily coaxed into running against Taft in the Republican primaries. Truman realized his own slim chances and bowed out. Eisenhower won a clear victory against Democrat Adlai Stevenson in the presidential elections. During the

Bradley served as the first chairman of the Joint Chiefs of Staff. Here is seen on a trip to Europe connected with the organization of NATO, along with with chief of naval operations Adm. Louis Denfield to the left and Air Force chief-of-staff Hoyt Vandenberg to the right. (MHI)

election campaign, Taft had used the policies of Bradley's JCS as a cudgel against Eisenhower. Ike had agreed to make changes in the Department of Defense, but these were undertaken in conjunction with Bradley. Bradley himself wanted to retire, and, in view of an unofficial understanding that he would be succeeded by an officer from another branch, Adm. Arthur Radford was selected to replace him as JCS chairman. The Army chief-of-staff position went to Matthew Ridgway. Bradley formally stepped down in August 1953.

In retirement, Bradley enjoyed his avocations of horseracing and college football. He held a number of honorary corporate positions, including chairman of the board of the Bulova Watch Company from 1958 to 1973. After his wife's death in 1965, he remarried in 1966. During the Vietnam War, he served as a special advisor on President Lyndon Johnson's team of "Wise Men." Bradley's attitudes on the Vietnam War were firmly on the hawkish side, and he was opposed to a withdrawal from Vietnam. Bradley suffered from ill health in his later years, and lived at the William Beaumont Army Medical Center near Ft. Bliss in Texas before dying of heart problems on April 8, 1981, at the age of 88. He is buried at Arlington National Cemetery outside Washington, DC.

Bradley confers with the other senior Army commanders on April 2, 1948. They include from left to right (front row) Thomas Hanky (Fourth Army Area); Omar Bradley (Army chief-of-staff); Mark Clark (Sixth Army Area); (upper row) Courtney Hodges (First Army Area); Walton Walker (Fifth Army Area), Leonard Gerow (Second Army Area), and Alvan Gillem (Third Army Area). (MHI)

INSIDE THE MIND

Bradley's views on future warfare were inspired by personal study as much as the Army's educational system. As a teenager, he had read avidly about America's early wars, with the usual focus on the French and Indian War, the Revolutionary War, and, most importantly, the Civil War. His West Point education had only cursory teaching on military history, but his appointment to West Point in 1921 gave him more opportunity to study the American art of war. Even though the post-World War I US Army focused on the lessons and tactics of the 1914–18 trench war, Bradley became convinced that the Civil War, and in particular the campaigns of William Sherman, offered a better template for future war. During his assignment to the advanced course at the Infantry School in 1924, he found the school curriculum to be an eye-opening revelation, with a great deal of attention paid to "open warfare" of the Civil War variety in spite of the Army's new focus on the lessons of 1914–18. At the same time, he was troubled by the failure of the school to integrate the impact of the tank and aircraft on the modern battlefield better. Bradley was becoming increasingly convinced that mechanization was the future of warfare.

His battalion command in Hawaii shaped Bradley's signature command style. He was adamant that commanders must develop an instinctive feel for terrain as an essential underpinning of infantry tactics, and he used both maps and three-dimensional sand tables both for his own education as well as the instruction of his subordinate commanders. This fascination with terrain study led to one of his aphorisms that commanders needed to examine tactical problems from the perspective of the enemy. Bradley was never a devotee of intelligence on enemy forces, but rather he meant that a commander needed to step back and examine the perspective from the enemy's side to better appreciate possible enemy reactions. While this approach had its merits, it also had its pitfalls as was so evident in the Ardennes, where Bradley's assessment of likely German intentions was badly skewed by his judgment of the inherent shortcomings of an attack through the Ardennes in the winter.

Bradley's academic appointment to the Command and General Staff School at Ft. Leavenworth helped him to better appreciate the professional aspects of staff planning and the formal Army approaches to tactics and doctrine. He found the courses to be conventional and too formulaic. At the same time, he appreciated that a commander could only adopt unconventional and more suitable tactics if well versed in the predictable and expected responses to tactical problems. Bradley was much more comfortable with the lessons promoted by George C. Marshall at the Infantry School in the late 1930s, with their accent on the war of maneuver. Bradley became one of the US Army's foremost trainers, spending 13 of his 23 years during the inter-war period in training posts at the Infantry School and West Point. His critical approach was to teach young officers self-reliance in making their tactical decisions, so that they did not depend on excessively detailed instructions from superior officers.

Bradley was very much the product of the inter-war US Army, and he was an enthusiastic proponent of the reformist tradition of Marshall and others. He was an early advocate of combined-arms doctrine, and he generally felt that most veterans of the American Expeditionary Force in France in 1918 were too complacent about the lessons from World War I, and that technology was likely to reverse the polarities of offense and defense in future wars.

Bradley was never a maverick and he generally felt uncomfortable with generals who were outside the mainstream, like Patton and "Terrible Terry Allen." If Bradley had been in charge, Patton would probably have been denied command of the Third US Army in 1944. Although Bradley tried to emulate Marshall's hard-nosed practice of liberally relieving subordinates due to poor performance, his bark was worse than his bite. In his memoirs, Bradley claimed credit for relieving Terry Allen from his 1st Infantry Division command on Sicily; the record would suggest that this was already in the works owing to Eisenhower and Patton's concern over his exhaustion. Bradley was often lenient with other commanders, such as his friend Courtney Hodges in spite of his questionable performance in the Ardennes.

Bradley was not hesitant to have divisional commanders relieved, but this was usually done by the lower field army and corps commands.

As a field commander in World War II Bradley was typical of most US infantry commanders, preferring a cautious approach that relied heavily on firepower. He proved to be quite comfortable in the integration of tanks and mechanized forces into contemporary tactics, and his major offensive campaigns, such as Operations *Cobra*, *Queen*, and *Voyage*, all involved the bold use of combined arms with a heavy reliance on both air power and tanks. In spite of the obvious problems with airborne forces on Sicily, Bradley was one of the most forceful advocates of the airborne operations connected to Operation *Overlord*. However, he showed reluctance to conduct airborne operations after the fiascos on D-Day and the Operation *Market-Garden* defeat. German commanders generally assessed him as being more conservative than other officers such as Patton, but then German commanders frequently misunderstood the intentions of several of his key plans. Bradley himself felt that his style put more emphasis on a solid grounding in logistics than Patton's plans. Bradley was not so self-centered as to reject the suggestions of talented subordinates. The plans for the race to the Seine originated in Patton's Third US Army, but Bradley took up the scheme with enthusiasm in promoting it with Eisenhower. After his experiences with Patton in Tunisia and Sicily, he tried to avoid micro-managing his subordinate commanders. Bradley was very much an "organization man," thoroughly inculcated in the ways of the US Army, especially as preached by George C. Marshall. As a result, he reflected the virtues and vices of his institution.

A LIFE IN WORDS

Bradley authored two books about his role in World War II. Published in 1951, *A Soldier's Story* followed Eisenhower's own account of the war years, *Crusade in Europe*. It was written while Bradley was still chairman of the Joint Chiefs of Staff. This book is not a full autobiography, but his personal view of the war years. It is widely believed that the book was at least partly ghost-written by his longtime aide, Chet Hansen. Regardless of the details of authorship, it certainly reflects Bradley's views of fellow commanders and the many controversies of the European campaigns. Bradley's second book, *A General's Life*, was published shortly after his death in 1983. This full-length autobiography was mainly the work of his collaborator, the noted American historian Clay Blair. It was based on Blair's extensive interviews with Bradley, as well as his own extensive historical research.

Bradley has not attracted as much attention by historians as Eisenhower, Patton, or MacArthur. Bradley's taciturn professionalism lacked the drama, egocentricity, and operatic exuberance of more theatrical commanders like Patton, Montgomery, and MacArthur. On the other hand, Bradley has fared better than his nearest American counterpart, Jacob Devers, commander of the 6th Army Group, who lacks an autobiography or a full-length biography. In this respect, Bradley is actually closer to the mainstream of senior American commanders who generally avoided the limelight. Four of the five US field army commanders in the ETO – Simpson, Hodges, Patch, and Gerow – are all virtually unknown to the general audience; only Patton has escaped anonymity.

Commanders who modeled themselves in the heroic mode of command, such as Patton, sought public attention. This is especially evident in the iconography of war. When combing through the US Army official photograph collection, it is impossible to miss the dozens of Patton photos; photos of Bradley on Sicily are almost totally absent, and the ones used in this book came from the personal collection of an officer on Bradley's staff and not from the official collection. The US Army Signal Corps photograph collection from World War II, now kept at Record Group 111-SC at the National Archives and Records Administration at College Park, Maryland, provides further evidence of Bradley's unassuming style. There are separate collections of photos of Eisenhower, MacArthur, Clark, and Patton, and even collections for lesser commanders such as Ridgway and Van Fleet. There is no Bradley collection. Bradley's First US Army Headquarters and his later 12th Army Group Headquarters did not have a press office permanently attached until February 1945, and most official photos of Bradley prior to 1945 were taken when Bradley was caught visiting other commanders.

FURTHER READING

US Army reports

12th Army Group, Report of Operations: Final After Action Report (1946)
First United States Army Report of Operations 1 August 1944 to 22 February 1945 (1946)
Third Army, Report of Operations, August 1944–May 1945 (1946)
To Bizerte with the II Corps: 23 April–13 May 1943 (1943)

Books

Alexrod, Alan, *Bradley* (Palgrave Macmillan: 2008)
Bradley, Omar, *A Soldier's Story* (Henry Holt: 1951)
Bradley, Omar, and Blair, Clay, *A General's Life* (Simon and Schuster: 1983)
Crosswell, D. K. R., *Beetle: The Life of General Walter Bedell Smith* (University Press of Kentucky: 2011)
English, John, *Patton's Peers: The Forgotten Allied Field Army Commanders of the Western Front 1944–45* (Stackpole: 2009)
Hogan, David, *A Command Post at War: First Army Headquarters in Europe, 1943–1945* (Center for Military History: 2000)
Jordan, Jonathan, *Brothers, Rivals, Victors: Eisenhower, Patton, Bradley and the Partnership that Drove the Allied Conquest in Europe* (NAL Caliber: 2011)
Weigley, Russell, *Eisenhower's Lieutenants: The Campaigns of France and Germany 1944–45* (Indiana University Press: 1981)

INDEX